MEET ME IN THE WORD: VOLUME 3

A DEVOTIONAL FOR COUPLES

MEET ME IN THE WORD
BOOK 3

JOHN O'MALLEY

To my wife, Kimberly, who sustained me in all seasons of our marriage journey with her meek and quiet spirit and love.

In the heart of my heart, I will always love you!

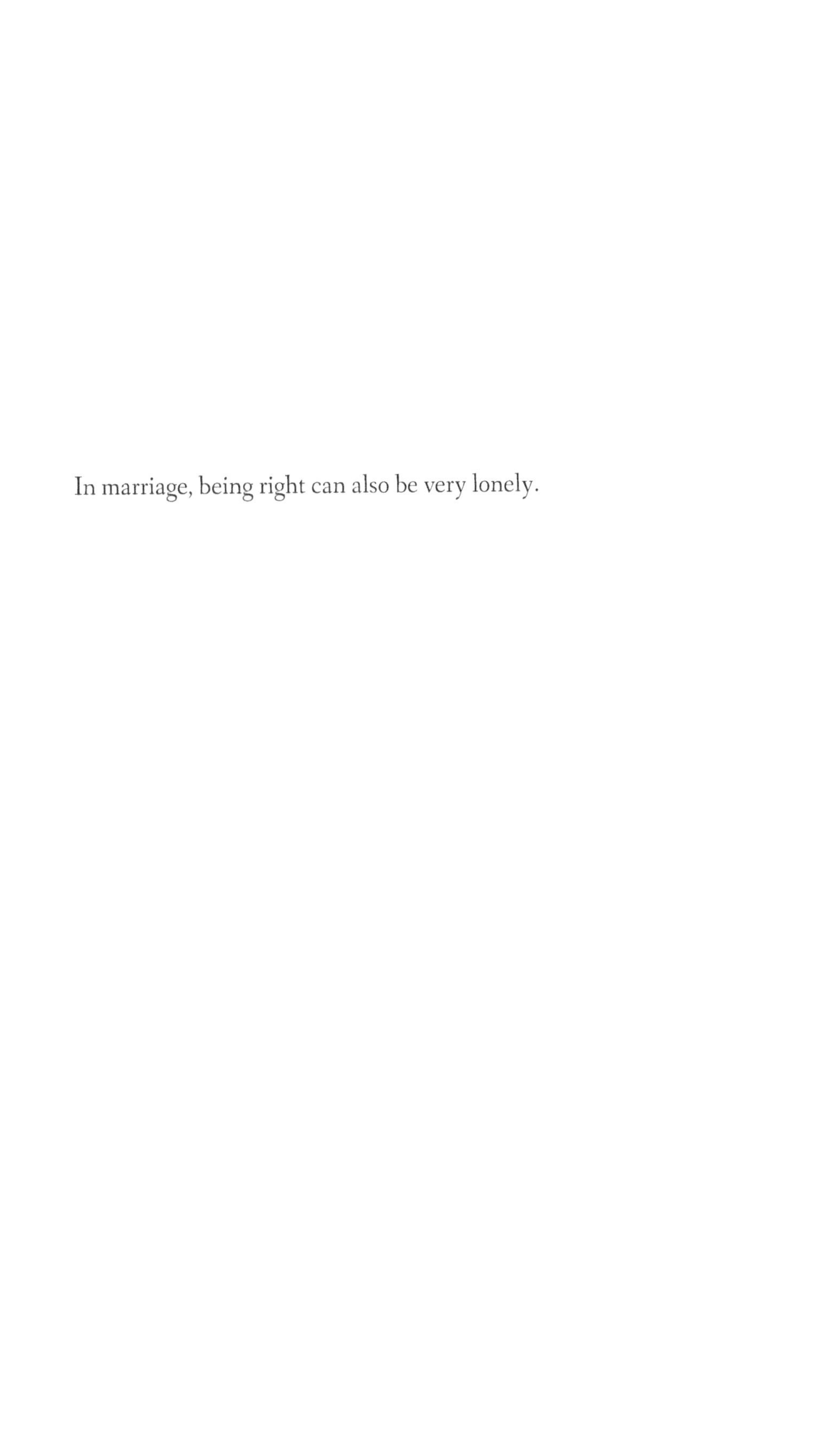

In marriage, being right can also be very lonely.

LETTER TO THE READER

Dear Reader,

This book is not just about practical advice for marriage but an invitation to deepen your relationship with God and your spouse through His Word.

Every devotion in this book explores the timeless wisdom of Scripture, applying God's truth to real-life situations couples face daily. From communication breakdowns to financial disagreements, from intimacy struggles to unmet expectations, this book offers insights from the Bible to help you build a more robust, Christ-centered marriage.

As you read through these pages, my hope and prayer is that you will gain biblical knowledge and discover new ways to love and serve your spouse, reflecting Christ's love in your home. May the Lord meet you in His Word, refresh your heart, and strengthen your marriage as you journey through this book together.

Yours for the harvest,

John O'Malley

WHY I WROTE THIS DEVOTIONAL

For years, Kim would opine about devotionals for couples. The writings were either too weak, too soft, or too disappointing.

We would find devotionals weak or unsuitable. We did not prefer their translation. We did not like how the verses were used; they were out of context. We did not care for the lack of biblical authority to edify the biblical roles in marriage as complementarianists.

So, after years of teaching marriage conferences, retreats, and counseling with couples, I felt like it was time to take all I studied, taught, and preached and write Meet Me in the Word.

We wanted a devotional to guide couples into the Word of God, help them grow spiritually, strengthen their marriage, and prepare them to disciple others.

Ultimately, Kim and I wanted a devotional we would use. I began with six core elements to make the devotional genuinely trans-formative:

We believed there should be a Devotional on Relationship Building

- At the heart of our devotional is the desire for couples to meet together in the Word. Not only will this help your relationship with each other, but it also draws you two closer to God. Each entry in the devotional:
  - It invites you to explore biblical passages that reflect God's design for marriage.
  - It prompts you to discuss personal applications of the Word in their relationship.
  - Encourages individual reflection and shared conversation.

We Decided to Make the Devotional both Practical and Intentional

- Creating a habit of daily Bible reading and prayer is essential for spiritual growth. For couples, this habit builds intimacy and fosters unity in their walk with God. We included relevant biblical passages in each lesson, balancing practical advice with theological insights.

We structured each devotional with these elements:

- **Scripture Focus**: Begins with a Bible passage addressing the topic.
- **A Shared Moment:** Illustrates a scenario in marriage to help teach a principle.
- **Scripture Exposition:** Explains the Scriptural principle from the passage.
- **Discussion Prompt**: This prompt offers a question or thought for you two to discuss together (*e.g., "How can*

we practice forgiveness as Jesus taught us in Matthew 6:14-15?").

- **Prayer Focus**: This provides a short prayer prompt. You can pray together, asking God to deepen your connection.
- **Action Step**: This step challenges you with a practical action for the day (*e.g., "Today, practice active listening with your spouse, focusing on their needs."*).
- **Marriage Minute:** Focuses on a principle or lesson from the marriage conferences we teach. We applied this to the four stages of marriage. Those stages are:
  - **Love's New Chapter** — Couples who are newly married. *0-10 years*
  - **Love in Motion** — Couples who have been married for a while. *11-20 years*
  - **Love's Legacy** — Couples who have been married for years. *20-30 years*
  - **Legendary Lovebirds** — Couples who have been married for decades. *40 years or more*

We Emphasized Spiritual Growth as a Journey

- The goal of the devotional is long-term spiritual transformation.
- We wanted each devotional to be your stepping stone in their journey, not just a one-time activity.
- We want you to understand that growing together in Christ means:
  - **Learning to disciple others**: We want this devotional to prepare you as a couple to grow yourselves and eventually help others. Each devotional could include an outreach element, such as praying for other couples or family members.

- ○ **Building a foundation in the Word**: Over time, couples should see their time in Scripture as the bedrock of their marriage, reinforcing their commitment to God and each other.

We Infused the Devotional with Encouragement and Hope

Every entry in the devotional should lift you as a couple, reminding you that your marriage reflects Christ's love for the church. Even when dealing with challenging topics like forgiveness, trust, or unmet expectations, the tone is always one of hope and grace, grounded in the truth of Scripture.

We Emphasized the Power of God's Word

- The title, *Meet Me in the Word*, captures the essence of our vision. The Word of God is the meeting place where couples connect with each other and God Himself.
- Every solution, strengthening moment, and growth point comes from Scripture, not human effort. Your meeting in the Word becomes a powerful act of inviting God into the center of your marriage.

LOVE'S JOURNEY IN THE MARRIAGE MINUTE

A unique feature of each devotion is **The Marriage Minute** section at the end of every chapter.

The *Marriage Minute* is my favorite part. I wrote these short, impactful reflections to distill the critical lessons about marriage into bite-sized truths that can be immediately applied to everyday life.

Each *Marriage Minute* offers practical, scripture-based wisdom in a concise format. It empowers couples to focus on one key takeaway each day and provides a sense of reassurance and guidance.

The *Marriage Minute* sections emphasize small, intentional actions that can transform a marriage and instill a sense of hope and inspiration. From cultivating kindness in communication to rediscovering emotional intimacy and handling conflict with grace, these moments of reflection help couples practice the chapter's teachings, reinforcing biblical principles with real-life applications.

I wrote an application for every season of marriage. I divided the season of marriage with the idea of Love's Journey. I chose to call these milestones:

- **Love's New Chapter** — Couples who are newly married. *0-10 years*
- **Love in Motion** — Couples who have been married for a while. *11-20 years*
- **Love's Legacy** — Couples who have been married for years. *20-30 years*
- **Legendary Lovebirds** — Couples who have been married for decades. *40 years or more*

Look for your milestone each day and see what inspiration or conversation there is for you in your current season of life.

Kim and I married in 1986. We like using *Love's Legacy* and *Legendary Lovebirds* for our Marriage Minute.

SOURCES CITED

Throughout *Meet Me in the Word*, you will see I referenced publicly available studies and research from:

- Family Life
- Barna Research
- SYMBIS (Save Your Marriage Before It Starts)
- Focus on the Family

I appreciate the research of these groups. I am not endorsing their theology or their associations.

In the case of SYMBIS, I am certified by SYMBIS in marriage counseling.

MONTH THREE

REBUILDING AFTER FINANCIAL STRUGGLES: PHILIPPIANS 4:19 FOR TRUST IN GOD'S PROVISION

SCRIPTURE FOCUS:

"But my God shall supply all your need according to his riches in glory by Christ Jesus." – Philippians 4:19

A Shared Moment:

James and Kelly had faced a difficult financial season due to unexpected medical expenses and a job loss. Tensions had risen as they worried about how they would make ends meet. According to research from Family Life, financial stress is one of the leading causes of conflict in marriage. James and Kelly realized they needed to trust in God's provision and work together to rebuild their financial foundation.

Scripture Exposition:

Philippians 4:19 is a powerful reminder that God will supply all of our needs according to His riches in glory. In marriage, financial struggles can create significant stress, but this verse assures us that God is our Provider. Trusting in His provision allows couples to find peace, even in times of financial difficulty. When spouses come together to trust in God and work as a team, they can rebuild their financial situation and strengthen their marriage in the process. God's provision is not just material but also emotional and spiritual, helping couples grow stronger together.

Discussion Prompt:

Are financial struggles causing stress in your marriage? How can you both trust in God's provision and work together to rebuild your financial foundation? Discuss how Philippians 4:19 encourages you to rely on God to supply all your needs.

Prayer Focus:

Father, we thank You for being our Provider and for the promise that You will supply all our needs. Help us to trust in Your provision during times of financial struggle and to work together as a team in our marriage. Teach us to rely on Your wisdom and guidance in managing our finances, and to trust that You will provide for us in every way. We are grateful for Your faithfulness. Amen.

Action Step:

Today, review your financial situation together and pray for God's wisdom and provision. Create a plan to manage your finances, trusting that God will guide you and provide for your needs.

Marriage Minute #61: Building a Partnership, Not a Competition

Marriage is a partnership, not a competition. Ecclesiastes 4:9-10 teaches us, "Two are better than one; because they have a good reward for their labour. For if they fall, the one will lift up his fellow." In a healthy marriage, both partners work together toward common goals, supporting and uplifting one another, rather than competing for control or recognition.

Building a partnership means recognizing that you are on the same team. It involves celebrating each other's successes, sharing responsibilities, and offering help when one person is struggling. A marriage that operates as a partnership fosters unity, trust, and a deep sense of shared purpose. It's about lifting each other up, not tearing each other down.

Key Truth:

> Building a partnership in marriage fosters unity and trust, allowing both spouses to support each other and work together toward common goals.

Love's New Chapter:
As newlyweds, focus on building a strong partnership by working together, sharing responsibilities, and supporting each other's goals. This teamwork will lay the foundation for a successful marriage.

Love in Motion:
For couples married a while, it's easy to fall into the trap of competing for control or recognition. Recommit to working as a team, supporting each other's strengths and celebrating each other's successes.

Love's Legacy:

After many years of marriage, your partnership has likely been a key factor in your success. Continue to foster unity by working together toward common goals and offering help when one person is struggling.

Legendary Lovebirds:

For those married for decades, your strong partnership is a testimony to the power of teamwork in marriage. Keep modeling this for others, showing that when both partners work together, the marriage thrives.

HEALING FROM EMOTIONAL WOUNDS: PSALM 147:3 FOR GOD'S RESTORATION

SCRIPTURE FOCUS:

"He healeth the broken in heart, and bindeth up their wounds." – Psalm 147:3

A Shared Moment:

Tanya had been carrying emotional wounds from past relationships that affected her ability to fully open up to her husband, Ryan. Ryan, too, had his own emotional scars from difficult experiences. According to SYMBIS, unresolved emotional wounds can create barriers in marriage, preventing true intimacy. Tanya and Ryan realized they needed to turn to God for healing and work together to rebuild trust and emotional connection.

Scripture Exposition:

Psalm 147:3 reminds us that God is the ultimate healer of the brokenhearted. Emotional wounds, whether from past relationships or experiences, can hinder intimacy in marriage, but God promises to heal and bind up those wounds. When couples turn to God for healing, they open the door to emotional restoration and deeper connection. Healing is not always immediate, but as couples work through their wounds together, they find strength in God's presence and the support of their spouse. God's healing power is essential for emotional wholeness in marriage.

Discussion Prompt:

Have emotional wounds from the past affected your marriage? How can you both seek God's healing and work together to rebuild emotional intimacy? Discuss how Psalm 147:3 encourages you to trust in God's power to heal your broken hearts and restore your marriage.

Prayer Focus:

Lord, we thank You for being the healer of our hearts and for binding up our wounds. Help us to turn to You for healing from any emotional scars, and teach us to support each other as we work toward emotional wholeness in our marriage. We are grateful for Your presence and healing power in our lives. Amen.

Action Step:

Today, have an open and honest conversation about any emotional wounds that have affected your marriage. Pray together for God's healing and commit to supporting each other through the process of restoration.

Marriage Minute #62: Practicing Self-Control

Self-control is essential for maintaining peace and harmony in marriage. Proverbs 25:28 warns, "He that hath no rule over his own spirit is like a city that is broken down, and without walls." In marriage, practicing self-control means being mindful of your words, actions, and emotions, especially during moments of frustration or conflict.

Self-control involves choosing to respond with patience instead of anger, keeping a calm tone, and refraining from impulsive actions or hurtful words. It helps prevent misunderstandings and conflicts from escalating. When both partners practice self-control, it fosters a safe, respectful environment where love can grow, and disagreements can be resolved calmly.

Key Truth:

> Practicing self-control in marriage fosters peace, respect, and emotional security, allowing both spouses to navigate conflict with grace and patience.

Love's New Chapter:

As newlyweds, learning to practice self-control in difficult moments will set a strong foundation for your marriage. Be intentional about managing your emotions and choosing to respond with patience and love.

Love in Motion:

For couples married a while, tensions can sometimes flare in stressful situations. Recommit to practicing self-control, keeping your emotions in check, and responding to disagreements with grace.

Love's Legacy:

After many years of marriage, self-control has likely played a key role in keeping peace during conflicts. Continue to practice this discipline, knowing that it strengthens your marriage and builds mutual respect.

Legendary Lovebirds:

For those married for decades, your ability to practice self-control has likely been a source of harmony in your relationship. Keep modeling this for others, showing that self-control is vital for a peaceful, loving marriage that stands the test of time.

SCRIPTURE FOCUS:

"Trust in the Lord with all thine heart; and lean not unto thine own understanding. In all thy ways acknowledge him, and he shall direct thy paths." – Proverbs 3:5-6

A Shared Moment:

Sarah and Tom had been debating a big decision—whether to move to a new city for a job opportunity. The weight of the decision had caused stress and disagreement between them. According to research by Family Life, making major life decisions is one of the top sources of tension in marriage. Sarah and Tom realized that they needed to seek God's guidance together, trusting Him to direct their steps.

Scripture Exposition:

Proverbs 3:5-6 encourages believers to trust in the Lord with all their hearts and not to rely on their own understanding. In marriage, when facing major life decisions, it's easy to become overwhelmed by uncertainty. This verse reminds couples to acknowledge God in all their ways and trust that He will direct their paths. When both partners seek God's guidance in decision-making, they find peace and unity in the process. Trusting in God's wisdom ensures that decisions are made with His plan in mind, rather than personal desires or fears.

Discussion Prompt:

Are you currently facing a big decision in your marriage? How can you both seek God's guidance and trust Him to direct your steps? Discuss how Proverbs 3:5-6 encourages you to rely on God's wisdom when making important decisions.

Prayer Focus:

Father, we thank You for the promise that You will direct our paths when we trust in You. Help us to seek Your guidance in every decision we make, especially in the big moments. Teach us to rely on Your wisdom rather than our own understanding, and guide us toward unity and peace in our marriage. We are grateful for Your direction and love. Amen.

Action Step:

Today, take time to pray together about any major decisions you're facing. Trust God to guide your steps and commit to making decisions together, acknowledging His wisdom above all else.

Marriage Minute #63: Sharing a Common Vision

A shared vision helps couples stay united and focused on common goals. Amos 3:3 asks, "Can two walk together, except they be agreed?" In marriage, it's essential to have a common vision for your life together—a shared set of goals, values, and dreams that guide your decisions and keep you working as a team.

This vision may include spiritual goals, financial plans, family aspirations, or personal growth. It's important to revisit your shared vision regularly, ensuring that both partners are aligned in their desires for the future. When both spouses are working toward the same vision, it fosters unity, purpose, and a sense of partnership in marriage.

Key Truth:

> Sharing a common vision in marriage fosters unity and purpose, helping both spouses work together toward their shared goals and dreams.

Love's New Chapter:
As newlyweds, take time to discuss your shared vision for the future. Align your goals, values, and dreams so that you can work together as a team, building a strong foundation for your marriage.

Love in Motion:
For couples married a while, life's busyness can sometimes pull you in different directions. Revisit your shared vision, and make sure that both of you are still aligned in your goals and working toward the same future.

Love's Legacy:
After many years of marriage, your shared vision has likely been a guiding force in your relationship. Continue to discuss your future

dreams and goals, ensuring that you are still working together toward a common purpose.

Legendary Lovebirds:

For those married for decades, your shared vision has likely helped you stay united through many seasons of life. Keep modeling this for younger couples, showing that a common vision creates a strong, enduring partnership.

SCRIPTURE FOCUS:

"For God hath not given us the spirit of fear; but of power, and of love, and of a sound mind." – 2 Timothy 1:7

A Shared Moment:

Kevin and Rachel were both ambitious in their careers, but they struggled with the fear of failure, especially when things didn't go as planned. This fear began to affect their marriage, making them hesitant to take risks or pursue new opportunities. According to research from Barna, the fear of failure can create anxiety and hesitation in marriage. Kevin and Rachel realized they needed to turn to God's promise of power and a sound mind to overcome their fears and move forward in faith.

Scripture Exposition:

2 Timothy 1:7 reminds us that God has not given us a spirit of fear, but of power, love, and a sound mind. In marriage, when both partners struggle with fear of failure, it can create a sense of paralysis

or anxiety. However, God calls us to live in His power and love, trusting that He equips us for every challenge. By relying on God's strength and wisdom, couples can overcome their fears and pursue God's plan for their lives and marriage with confidence. God's love casts out fear, enabling couples to face challenges with courage and unity.

Discussion Prompt:

Have you or your spouse ever struggled with the fear of failure? How can you both rely on God's power and love to overcome this fear in your marriage? Discuss how 2 Timothy 1:7 encourages you to trust in God's strength and live with courage rather than fear.

Prayer Focus:

Father, we thank You for the power, love, and sound mind You have given us. Help us to overcome any fears of failure in our marriage, trusting in Your strength and wisdom. Teach us to rely on Your love and power, facing every challenge with courage and faith. We are grateful for Your presence and guidance. Amen.

Action Step:

Today, identify one area where fear of failure has held you back. Pray together for God's courage and strength, and commit to moving forward in faith, trusting that God has equipped you for success.

Marriage Minute #64: Learning to Laugh Together

Laughter is a powerful way to connect with your spouse and bring joy to your marriage. Proverbs 17:22 reminds us, "A merry heart doeth good like a medicine." In marriage, laughter can help relieve stress, lighten difficult situations, and create a bond of shared joy and playfulness.

Learning to laugh together means finding humor in everyday life, sharing jokes, and enjoying lighthearted moments. Laughter fosters emotional intimacy and strengthens the relationship, making it easier to face challenges together. A marriage filled with laughter is one that thrives on joy and positivity.

Key Truth:

> Laughter in marriage fosters emotional intimacy and joy, helping both spouses navigate life's challenges with a positive outlook.

Love's New Chapter:

As newlyweds, take time to laugh together and enjoy each other's company. Share jokes, watch something funny, and create moments of joy that strengthen your bond.

Love in Motion:

For couples married a while, life's demands can sometimes take away the fun. Be intentional about bringing laughter back into your marriage by finding reasons to smile, laugh, and enjoy each other's company.

Love's Legacy:

After many years of marriage, laughter may have played a key role in helping you navigate life's challenges. Continue to laugh together, finding humor and joy in the small moments of daily life.

. . .

Legendary Lovebirds:

For those married for decades, your ability to laugh together has likely been a sustaining force in your relationship. Keep modeling this for others, showing that laughter brings joy and resilience to a long-lasting marriage.

SCRIPTURE FOCUS:

"For where two or three are gathered together in my name, there am I in the midst of them." – Matthew 18:20

A Shared Moment:

After years of marriage, Emily and Jake realized that they had drifted apart spiritually. While they prayed individually, they rarely prayed together as a couple. According to SYMBIS research, couples who pray together report stronger emotional and spiritual connections. Emily and Jake knew that prioritizing prayer as a couple was essential for deepening their bond and inviting God's presence into their relationship.

Scripture Exposition:

Matthew 18:20 promises that where two or three gather in God's name, He is present among them. In marriage, prayer is a powerful tool for connecting not only with God but also with each other. When couples prioritize praying together, they create an opportunity for God to work in their relationship, guiding their steps, healing wounds, and strengthening their bond. By making prayer a regular part of their marriage, couples invite God's presence into their home and relationship, building a strong foundation of faith and unity.

Discussion Prompt:

Do you and your spouse pray together regularly? How can you both make prayer a priority in your marriage, inviting God's presence into your relationship? Discuss how Matthew 18:20 encourages you to gather together in prayer, trusting that God is with you.

Prayer Focus:

Lord, we thank You for the promise that You are with us when we gather in Your name. Help us to prioritize prayer in our marriage, seeking Your presence and guidance daily. Teach us to pray together with faith, trusting that You are at work in our relationship. We are grateful for Your love and the peace You bring to our marriage. Amen.

Action Step:

Today, set aside time to pray together, even if it's just for a few minutes. Make it a habit to pray as a couple, seeking God's presence and guidance in your marriage.

Marriage Minute #65: The Power of Unity

Unity in marriage is about working together, sharing responsibilities, and supporting each other through every season. Ecclesiastes 4:12 teaches, "And if one prevail against him, two shall withstand him; and a threefold cord is not quickly broken." Unity means facing challenges as a team, celebrating successes together, and making decisions that reflect the best interests of both partners.

When both spouses are united in their goals, values, and actions, the marriage becomes stronger. Unity fosters a sense of partnership, trust, and mutual respect. It also creates a foundation of strength, allowing the couple to weather life's storms together.

Key Truth:

> Unity in marriage strengthens the bond between spouses, creating a partnership built on trust, respect, and shared purpose.

Love's New Chapter:
As newlyweds, focus on building unity by making decisions together and supporting each other's goals. This unity will create a strong foundation for a lasting, successful marriage.

Love in Motion:
For couples married a while, unity can sometimes be challenged by life's pressures. Recommit to working as a team, facing challenges together, and making decisions that reflect your shared goals and values.

Love's Legacy:
After many years of marriage, unity has likely been a key factor in your lasting relationship. Continue to foster unity by supporting each other and working together toward your common goals.

.   .   .

Legendary Lovebirds:

For those married for decades, your unity has likely been a source of strength in your marriage. Keep modeling this for younger couples, showing that unity is the foundation of a strong, resilient relationship that can withstand any challenge.

CULTIVATING PATIENCE IN MARRIAGE: GALATIANS 5:22-23 FOR THE FRUIT OF THE SPIRIT

SCRIPTURE FOCUS:

"But the fruit of the Spirit is love, joy, peace, longsuffering, gentleness, goodness, faith, meekness, temperance: against such there is no law." – Galatians 5:22-23

A Shared Moment:

Sara and Paul found that their patience was wearing thin. Whether it was small annoyances or larger disagreements, they seemed to snap at each other more frequently. According to research from Family Life, impatience can lead to frustration and resentment in marriage. Sara and Paul knew they needed to cultivate the fruit of patience, allowing the Holy Spirit to work in their hearts and transform their attitudes.

Scripture Exposition:

Galatians 5:22-23 lists the fruit of the Spirit, including patience (longsuffering), as essential qualities that should be evident in the lives of believers. In marriage, patience is key to maintaining peace, understanding, and love. By allowing the Holy Spirit to cultivate the fruit of patience in our hearts, we become more equipped to handle conflicts, frustrations, and everyday challenges with grace. Couples who rely on the Holy Spirit to produce patience will experience greater peace and unity, reflecting Christ's love in their relationship.

Discussion Prompt:

Have you ever struggled with impatience in your marriage? How can you both allow the Holy Spirit to cultivate the fruit of patience in your relationship? Discuss how Galatians 5:22-23 encourages you to rely on God's Spirit to transform your hearts and attitudes.

Prayer Focus:

Father, we thank You for the fruit of the Spirit that You produce in our lives. Help us to cultivate patience in our marriage, relying on the Holy Spirit to transform our hearts and attitudes. Teach us to approach each other with grace, understanding, and love, reflecting the patience You have shown us. We are grateful for Your presence and guidance. Amen.

Action Step:

Today, make a conscious effort to practice patience in your interactions with your spouse. When you feel frustrated or impatient, take a deep breath and ask the Holy Spirit to fill you with His peace and understanding.

Marriage Minute #66: Creating a Culture of Peace

Creating a peaceful home is one of the greatest gifts you can give your spouse. Romans 12:18 encourages us, "If it be possible, as much as lieth in you, live peaceably with all men." In marriage, this means fostering an environment where love, respect, and understanding reign, and where conflict is resolved calmly and compassionately.

A culture of peace is built through kind words, patience, forgiveness, and a commitment to working through disagreements without anger or harshness. When both spouses prioritize peace, the home becomes a place of refuge, safety, and emotional security.

Key Truth:

> Creating a culture of peace in marriage fosters a loving, respectful environment where both spouses can thrive emotionally and spiritually.

Love's New Chapter:

As newlyweds, start building a peaceful home by committing to resolve conflicts with love and patience. Create a safe, calming environment where both of you feel respected and valued.

Love in Motion:

For couples married a while, life's stresses can sometimes disrupt the peace. Be intentional about fostering a culture of peace in your home by using kind words, practicing patience, and resolving conflicts quickly.

Love's Legacy:

After many years of marriage, peace has likely been a cornerstone of your relationship. Continue to create a peaceful home, where both partners feel safe, loved, and respected, even during difficult times.

.   .   .

Legendary Lovebirds:

For those married for decades, your peaceful home is likely a testament to the love and respect you've cultivated over the years. Keep modeling this for others, showing that peace is the foundation of a joyful, loving marriage.

FORGIVENESS AFTER A FIGHT: COLOSSIANS 3:13 FOR GRACE AND RESTORATION

SCRIPTURE FOCUS:

"Forbearing one another, and forgiving one another, if any man have a quarrel against any: even as Christ forgave you, so also do ye." – Colossians 3:13

A Shared Moment:

After a heated argument, both Leah and Ryan were hurt and upset. The harsh words spoken in the moment lingered, and neither of them knew how to move forward. According to research from Family Life, unresolved conflicts can create long-term damage in a marriage if forgiveness is not extended. Leah and Ryan knew they needed to forgive each other and work toward healing, just as Christ has forgiven them.

Scripture Exposition:

Colossians 3:13 calls believers to forgive one another, just as Christ has forgiven us. In marriage, forgiveness is essential for healing and restoration after a disagreement or fight. Holding on to bitterness or anger only causes further division, but when couples choose to forgive, they reflect the grace of God in their relationship. Forgiveness doesn't mean dismissing the hurt; it means choosing to let go of resentment and seeking restoration. God's grace empowers us to forgive and to rebuild trust and unity in our marriage.

Discussion Prompt:

Have you ever found it difficult to forgive after a fight? How can you both work toward forgiveness and healing, even in the midst of hurt? Discuss how Colossians 3:13 encourages you to extend grace and forgiveness to each other, just as Christ has forgiven you.

Prayer Focus:

Lord, we thank You for the forgiveness You have given us through Christ. Help us to extend that same grace and forgiveness to each other in our marriage, especially after disagreements or hurtful moments. Teach us to let go of resentment and to seek restoration, trusting in Your grace to heal our hearts. We are grateful for Your presence and peace. Amen.

Action Step:

Today, if there is any lingering hurt from a recent argument, take the first step toward forgiveness. Have an open conversation, seek to understand each other's feelings, and extend grace and forgiveness, letting God's healing work in your hearts.

Marriage Minute #67: Trusting God Together

A marriage built on trust in God is one that can withstand any challenge. Proverbs 3:5-6 reminds us, "Trust in the Lord with all thine heart; and lean not unto thine own understanding. In all thy ways acknowledge him, and he shall direct thy paths." Trusting God together means seeking His guidance in your marriage, praying for wisdom, and relying on His strength in times of difficulty.

When both spouses are committed to trusting God, it strengthens their bond and brings peace, knowing that He is in control. Trusting God together helps you make decisions that honor Him and each other, and it allows both partners to rely on His provision and guidance.

Key Truth:

Trusting God together strengthens your marriage by aligning your hearts with His will, bringing peace, wisdom, and direction to your relationship.

Love's New Chapter:

As newlyweds, build your marriage on trust in God. Pray together, seek His guidance, and rely on His wisdom as you make decisions for your life together.

Love in Motion:

For couples married a while, life's challenges can sometimes cause doubt. Recommit to trusting God together, praying for His wisdom and strength in every season of your marriage.

Love's Legacy:

After many years of marriage, trusting God together has likely helped you navigate many seasons. Continue to seek His guidance and rely on His provision, knowing that He is faithful to lead and sustain your marriage.

Legendary Lovebirds:

For those married for decades, your trust in God has likely been a constant source of strength. Keep modeling this trust for others, showing that when both spouses lean on God, they can weather any storm and enjoy a marriage built on a foundation of faith and reliance on Him.

DEALING WITH JEALOUSY IN MARRIAGE: James 3:16 for Peace and Unity

Scripture Focus:

"For where envying and strife is, there is confusion and every evil work." – James 3:16

A Shared Moment:

Rachel couldn't help but feel a twinge of jealousy when her husband, Mark, received praise at work or spent time with friends. While she trusted him, she struggled with feeling left out or overshadowed. According to SYMBIS research, jealousy can create insecurity and division in marriage if left unchecked. Rachel and Mark realized they needed to address the underlying issues of jealousy and work toward greater transparency and trust.

Scripture Exposition:

James 3:16 warns of the destructive nature of envy and strife, which can lead to confusion and conflict. In marriage, jealousy undermines trust and creates emotional distance between spouses. However, God calls us to live in peace and unity, not allowing jealousy to take root in our hearts. By addressing feelings of jealousy and fostering open communication, couples can work toward greater trust and connection. When we choose to live in the peace of Christ, we create a marriage that reflects His love and unity.

Discussion Prompt:

Has jealousy ever affected your marriage? How can you both address feelings of jealousy with openness and trust, working toward peace and unity? Discuss how James 3:16 encourages you to avoid envy and strife in your relationship, choosing peace instead.

Prayer Focus:

Father, we thank You for the peace You offer us through Christ. Help us to overcome any feelings of jealousy or insecurity in our marriage, choosing instead to trust each other and to live in unity. Teach us to communicate openly and to seek peace in every aspect of our relationship. We are grateful for Your love and guidance. Amen.

Action Step:

Today, if jealousy has caused tension in your marriage, have an honest conversation about it. Work together to rebuild trust and foster transparency, creating a foundation of peace and unity in your relationship.

Marriage Minute #68: The Importance of Rest in Marriage

In our fast-paced world, rest often takes a back seat to the demands of life. Yet, God commands us to rest. Mark 6:31 says, "And he said unto them, Come ye yourselves apart into a desert place, and rest a while." In marriage, prioritizing rest—both individually and together—is crucial for maintaining physical, emotional, and spiritual health.

Rest in marriage involves taking time away from the busyness of life to recharge, reflect, and reconnect with each other. It may mean scheduling time for relaxation, going on a retreat, or simply taking a break from daily routines to focus on your relationship. When both partners are rested, they are more present, patient, and loving.

Key Truth:

> Rest is essential in marriage for maintaining emotional and physical health, allowing both spouses to recharge and reconnect with one another.

Love's New Chapter:

As newlyweds, prioritize rest by setting aside time to recharge together. Whether it's a quiet weekend at home or a short getaway, taking time to rest will help you stay connected and refreshed in your marriage.

Love in Motion:

For couples married a while, life's demands can make rest seem like a luxury. Be intentional about carving out time to rest and recharge, knowing that it will benefit both your health and your relationship.

Love's Legacy:

After many years of marriage, you've likely learned the importance of rest. Continue to make time for relaxation and reflection, ensuring that your marriage stays strong and balanced.

Legendary Lovebirds:

For those married for decades, your ability to rest together has likely helped sustain your relationship. Keep modeling this for younger couples, showing that a marriage that prioritizes rest is one that thrives through every season.

BUILDING A LEGACY OF FAITH: DEUTERONOMY 6:6-7 FOR PASSING ON FAITH TO FUTURE GENERATIONS

SCRIPTURE FOCUS:

"And these words, which I command thee this day, shall be in thine heart: And thou shalt teach them diligently unto thy children, and shalt talk of them when thou sittest in thine house, and when thou walkest by the way, and when thou liest down, and when thou risest up." – Deuteronomy 6:6-7

A Shared Moment:

John and Emily wanted their children to grow up with a strong foundation of faith, but they sometimes struggled with how to integrate spiritual lessons into their everyday life. According to Family Life research, families that actively teach and model their faith are more likely to pass it on to future generations. John and Emily realized that building a legacy of faith required intentionality and consistency in teaching their children about God.

Scripture Exposition:

Deuteronomy 6:6-7 provides a clear command to diligently teach

God's Word to future generations. In marriage, couples have the unique opportunity to build a legacy of faith, not only for their own relationship but for their children and future generations. By integrating faith into daily conversations, routines, and decisions, couples create an environment where faith is lived out in a tangible way. God calls us to be intentional about passing on His Word, ensuring that it takes root in the hearts of our children and future generations.

Discussion Prompt:

How can you both work together to build a legacy of faith in your family? What steps can you take to teach and model your faith to your children or those around you? Discuss how Deuteronomy 6:6-7 encourages you to diligently pass on God's Word to future generations.

Prayer Focus:

Lord, we thank You for the opportunity to build a legacy of faith in our family. Help us to be diligent in teaching Your Word and living out our faith in everyday life. Teach us to model Your love and truth to our children and to pass on a strong foundation of faith to future generations. We are grateful for Your guidance and presence in our family. Amen.

Action Step:

Today, choose one way to intentionally incorporate faith into your daily routine. Whether it's reading Scripture together, praying as a family, or discussing God's Word during everyday moments, commit to passing on your faith to the next generation.

Marriage Minute #69: Forging a Strong Spiritual Bond

A strong spiritual bond in marriage is built on shared faith, prayer, and a commitment to growing together in Christ. Ecclesiastes 4:12 reminds us, "A threefold cord is not quickly broken." When both spouses are committed to nurturing their relationship with God, it strengthens the bond between them and creates a solid foundation for their marriage.

Forging a strong spiritual bond means praying together, studying Scripture, attending church, and seeking God's guidance as a couple. As you grow together spiritually, you will find that your love for each other deepens, and your ability to face challenges with grace and faith increases.

Key Truth:

A strong spiritual bond in marriage creates a foundation of faith, unity, and resilience, allowing both spouses to grow closer to each other and to God.

Love's New Chapter:

As newlyweds, begin building a strong spiritual bond by praying together and studying God's Word. This will create a foundation of faith that will carry you through the challenges of marriage.

Love in Motion:

For couples married a while, it's important to continue nurturing your spiritual bond. Make time for prayer and Bible study, ensuring that your relationship is grounded in faith and God's guidance.

. . .

Love's Legacy:

After many years of marriage, your spiritual bond has likely been a key factor in your success. Continue to grow together spiritually, seeking God's wisdom and relying on Him to guide your marriage.

Legendary Lovebirds:

For those married for decades, your strong spiritual bond is a testimony to others. Keep modeling this for younger couples, showing that a marriage rooted in faith is one that endures through all of life's seasons.

STRENGTHENING COMMUNICATION IN MARRIAGE: PROVERBS 18:21 FOR THE POWER OF WORDS

SCRIPTURE FOCUS:

"Death and life are in the power of the tongue: and they that love it shall eat the fruit thereof." – Proverbs 18:21

A Shared Moment:

Alex and Megan often found themselves miscommunicating, leading to arguments over small misunderstandings. They realized that the way they spoke to each other sometimes out of frustration—was causing more harm than they realized. According to research by Family Life, effective communication is one of the key pillars of a healthy marriage. Alex and Megan knew they needed to change how they used their words, choosing to speak life into their marriage instead of tearing each other down.

Scripture Exposition:

Proverbs 18:21 reminds us of the immense power our words carry—they can either bring life or death. In marriage, how we communicate has a profound impact on our relationship. Words of encouragement, kindness, and affirmation build up the marriage, while harsh, critical, or negative words can create emotional distance. God calls us to use our words to build each other up, reflecting His love in how we communicate. By choosing life-giving words, couples can foster understanding, intimacy, and growth in their relationship.

Discussion Prompt:

How do you communicate with your spouse—are your words building them up or tearing them down? How can you both work on speaking life into your marriage? Discuss how Proverbs 18:21 encourages you to choose your words carefully and use them to strengthen your relationship.

Prayer Focus:

Lord, we thank You for the power of words and for the ability to speak life into our marriage. Help us to use our words wisely, choosing to build each other up rather than tear down. Teach us to communicate with kindness, love, and understanding, reflecting Your grace in every conversation. We are grateful for Your wisdom and guidance. Amen.

Action Step:

Today, focus on speaking words of encouragement and affirmation to your spouse. Make an effort to communicate with love and patience, and avoid any negative or harsh language.

Marriage Minute #70: Maintaining a Sense of Adventure

Marriage is a lifelong journey, and part of keeping it exciting is maintaining a sense of adventure. Proverbs 16:9 says, "A man's heart deviseth his way: but the Lord directeth his steps." In marriage, embracing new experiences together keeps the relationship fresh and exciting, helping both partners grow and enjoy life's journey.

Adventure doesn't have to be grand or expensive. It could be exploring a new hobby, taking a spontaneous day trip, or trying something new together. What matters is that both partners are open to stepping outside of their comfort zones and making memories along the way. A sense of adventure strengthens the bond between spouses and keeps the relationship lively and fun.

Key Truth:

> Maintaining a sense of adventure in marriage fosters growth, excitement, and a deeper connection between spouses as they explore life's journey together.

Love's New Chapter:

As newlyweds, make a habit of embracing adventure early in your marriage. Try new things together, explore new places, and create memories that will strengthen your bond and add joy to your relationship.

Love in Motion:

For couples married a while, life's routines can sometimes dampen your sense of adventure. Reignite your curiosity by finding new experiences to share, whether it's a hobby, trip, or spontaneous activity.

. . .

Love's Legacy:

After many years of marriage, your shared adventures have likely played a key role in your relationship. Continue to seek out new experiences together, finding joy in discovering new parts of life with your spouse.

Legendary Lovebirds:

For those married for decades, your ability to embrace adventure together has likely kept your relationship vibrant and exciting. Keep modeling this for younger couples, showing that a sense of adventure brings energy and joy to a lifelong marriage.

RESTORING TRUST AFTER BETRAYAL: PROVERBS 28:13 FOR CONFESSION AND FORGIVENESS

"He that covereth his sins shall not prosper: but whoso confesseth and forsaketh them shall have mercy." – Proverbs 28:13

A Shared Moment:

After a painful betrayal, Kate and Ben struggled to rebuild trust in their marriage. The emotional scars ran deep, and both of them wondered if their relationship could ever be fully restored. According to SYMBIS research, betrayal can cause lasting damage if not addressed with honesty, confession, and forgiveness. Kate and Ben knew that the road to restoration would be difficult, but they committed to seeking God's mercy and healing together.

Scripture Exposition:

Proverbs 28:13 teaches the importance of confession and forsaking sin to receive mercy. In marriage, when trust is broken through betrayal, healing begins with honest confession and genuine repentance. Trying to cover up or deny wrongdoing only deepens the wound, but God's mercy is extended to those who confess and seek forgiveness. When both partners commit to healing through truth, forgiveness, and accountability, they can experience God's restorative power in their relationship. Trust may take time to rebuild, but God's grace makes restoration possible.

Discussion Prompt:

Has trust ever been broken in your marriage? How can you both work toward confession, forgiveness, and restoration? Discuss how Proverbs 28:13 encourages you to be honest with each other and to seek God's mercy in rebuilding trust.

Prayer Focus:

Father, we thank You for Your mercy and grace, even in the midst of our brokenness. Help us to confess any wrongs and to seek forgiveness in our marriage, trusting in Your power to restore what has been hurt. Teach us to walk in truth and accountability, allowing Your grace to heal our relationship. We are grateful for Your love and restoration. Amen.

Action Step:

If trust has been broken, take time to have an honest conversation about what happened. Seek forgiveness, offer grace, and commit to rebuilding trust with God's help.

Marriage Minute #71: Building Resilience Through Hardship

Every marriage will face challenges, but it's how you respond to those challenges that builds resilience. James 1:2-3 encourages us,

"My brethren, count it all joy when ye fall into divers temptations; Knowing this, that the trying of your faith worketh patience." In marriage, resilience means enduring hardships together, trusting God to strengthen your bond through every trial.

Resilience is built through prayer, patience, and a commitment to supporting each other no matter what life brings. It's about seeing trials as opportunities for growth, both as individuals and as a couple. When both partners trust God and lean on each other during difficult times, their marriage becomes stronger and more resilient.

Key Truth:

> Building resilience through hardship strengthens your marriage, allowing both spouses to grow in faith, trust, and unity during life's challenges.

Love's New Chapter:

As newlyweds, you may not yet have faced significant hardships, but learning to support each other in difficult times will strengthen your bond. Trust God to guide you through challenges, and lean on each other for support.

Love in Motion:

For couples married a while, life's hardships may have already tested your resilience. Continue to face challenges together with patience and prayer, knowing that God is using these trials to strengthen your relationship.

Love's Legacy:

After many years of marriage, resilience has likely played a key role in your ability to navigate life's ups and downs. Continue to trust God and support each other, knowing that your resilience has made your marriage stronger.

Legendary Lovebirds:

For those married for decades, your resilience through hardship has likely been a testimony to others. Keep modeling this for younger couples, showing that enduring trials together builds a marriage that can withstand any storm.

MAINTAINING UNITY IN MARRIAGE: EPHESIANS 4:3 FOR THE BOND OF PEACE

SCRIPTURE FOCUS:

"Endeavouring to keep the unity of the Spirit in the bond of peace." – Ephesians 4:3

A Shared Moment:

Amanda and Daniel had been going through a challenging season in their marriage. Differences in opinions on finances, parenting, and work-life balance had caused tension, and they found themselves arguing more than usual. According to Family Life research, maintaining unity in marriage requires effort, especially during difficult seasons. Amanda and Daniel realized they needed to work together to restore peace and unity, focusing on what truly matters.

Scripture Exposition:

Ephesians 4:3 encourages believers to work diligently to maintain unity through the bond of peace. In marriage, unity doesn't happen by accident; it requires intentional effort, grace, and a commitment to prioritizing peace over division. When couples strive for unity, they reflect the heart of God's design for marriage —a relationship built on love, mutual respect, and peace. By choosing to pursue peace in moments of conflict, couples strengthen their bond and create a marriage that reflects Christ's love and unity.

Discussion Prompt:

Have disagreements caused disunity in your marriage? How can you both work to maintain peace and unity in your relationship, even in difficult seasons? Discuss how Ephesians 4:3 encourages you to prioritize unity and work together toward a peaceful marriage.

Prayer Focus:

Lord, we thank You for the unity You desire for our marriage. Help us to work diligently to maintain peace and unity, even in challenging seasons. Teach us to prioritize each other, choosing love and grace over division. We are grateful for Your peace and for the strength You provide to keep our relationship united in You. Amen.

Action Step:

Today, focus on one area where there has been disunity in your marriage. Work together to find a solution that fosters peace and strengthens your unity, committing to pursue peace in all aspects of your relationship.

Marriage Minute #72: The Power of Affirmation

Affirmation is a simple yet powerful way to strengthen your marriage. Proverbs 16:24 reminds us, "Pleasant words are as an honeycomb, sweet to the soul, and health to the bones." In marriage, affirming your spouse through words of encouragement, appreciation, and love can uplift their spirit and deepen your connection.

Affirmations remind your spouse that they are valued, loved, and appreciated. Whether it's a compliment, a note of encouragement, or simply thanking them for their contributions, your words have the power to strengthen their confidence and build up your relationship. Affirmations are especially meaningful in difficult times, offering reassurance and support.

Key Truth:

> Affirming your spouse with words of love and encouragement strengthens your relationship, fostering emotional intimacy and building confidence.

Love's New Chapter:

As newlyweds, affirming your spouse early in your marriage sets the tone for a loving and supportive relationship. Take time each day to offer compliments and words of encouragement, creating an atmosphere of love and appreciation.

Love in Motion:

For couples married a while, affirmations can sometimes get lost in the busyness of life. Be intentional about offering words of encouragement and love, reminding your spouse that they are valued and appreciated.

Love's Legacy:

After many years of marriage, affirmations have likely played a key role in maintaining emotional intimacy. Continue to affirm your spouse, especially during challenging times, offering support and love through your words.

Legendary Lovebirds:

For those married for decades, your affirmations have likely strengthened your marriage over the years. Keep modeling this for others, showing that words of love and encouragement are essential for a lasting, fulfilling relationship.

TRUSTING GOD'S TIMING IN MARRIAGE: ECCLESIASTES 3:1 FOR PATIENCE AND PEACE

SCRIPTURE FOCUS:

"To every thing there is a season, and a time to every purpose under the heaven." – Ecclesiastes 3:1

A Shared Moment:

Mark and Anna had been praying for a breakthrough in their lives, whether in finances, health, or a new opportunity. Yet, they felt stuck, frustrated that things weren't happening in the time they had hoped. According to Family Life, many couples struggle with aligning their expectations with God's timing. Mark and Anna realized they needed to trust that God's timing was perfect, even if it didn't match their own.

Scripture Exposition:

Ecclesiastes 3:1 reminds us that there is a time and season for everything under heaven. In marriage, waiting on God's timing can be difficult, especially when it feels like prayers are unanswered or progress is slow. However, God's timing is perfect, and He works all things together for good. Trusting in God's plan means having patience and faith, even when circumstances seem uncertain. By leaning on God and trusting His timing, couples can experience peace, knowing that He is in control of every season of life.

Discussion Prompt:

Have you ever struggled with waiting for God's timing in your marriage? How can you both trust that God's timing is perfect, even when it feels delayed? Discuss how Ecclesiastes 3:1 encourages you to be patient and trust in God's plan for your marriage.

Prayer Focus:

Father, we thank You for Your perfect timing and for the promise that You are in control of every season. Help us to trust in Your plan for our marriage, even when we feel impatient or uncertain. Teach us to lean on You, knowing that Your timing is always good. We are grateful for Your wisdom and peace. Amen.

Action Step:

Today, talk about an area where you've been waiting on God's timing. Commit to praying together for patience and peace, trusting that God's timing is perfect in all things.

Marriage Minute #73: Embracing Seasons of Change

Marriage is a journey that goes through many seasons—some filled with joy, others with challenges. Ecclesiastes 3:1 tells us, "To every thing there is a season, and a time to every purpose under the heaven." In marriage, it's important to embrace these seasons of change, trusting that God has a purpose for each one.

Change is inevitable, whether it's related to careers, family, health, or personal growth. Embracing these changes together means being flexible, supporting each other through transitions, and trusting that God is guiding your steps. When both partners approach change with a spirit of unity and faith, the marriage grows stronger.

Key Truth:

> Embracing seasons of change in marriage fosters growth, trust, and unity, as both partners navigate life's transitions together with faith and flexibility.

Love's New Chapter:

As newlyweds, you are entering a new season of life together. Embrace the changes that come with marriage by supporting each other and trusting God to guide you through each transition.

Love in Motion:

For couples married a while, change may come in the form of new responsibilities or challenges. Approach these changes as a team, offering support and reassurance to one another as you navigate new seasons together.

Love's Legacy:

After many years of marriage, you've likely experienced many seasons of change. Continue to embrace each new season with grace, trusting that God is working in your marriage through every transition.

. . .

Legendary Lovebirds:

For those married for decades, your ability to navigate seasons of change together has likely been a source of strength. Keep modeling this for younger couples, showing that flexibility and trust in God are key to thriving through life's changes.

SCRIPTURE FOCUS:

"A soft answer turneth away wrath: but grievous words stir up anger." – Proverbs 15:1

A Shared Moment:

Whenever Emily brought up something that bothered her, James responded defensively, and their conversations quickly escalated into arguments. Both felt unheard and misunderstood. According to research by SYMBIS, learning to handle criticism in marriage with grace can prevent conflicts from escalating. Emily and James knew they needed to approach sensitive topics with gentleness, using soft words to communicate instead of harsh ones.

Scripture Exposition:

Proverbs 15:1 teaches the power of a soft answer to defuse anger, while harsh words stir up conflict. In marriage, criticism can often feel like an attack, but responding with gentleness helps to calm the situation and promote understanding. God calls us to communicate with grace and patience, especially in difficult conversations. By choosing soft words and a gentle spirit, couples can create an atmosphere of trust and openness, allowing for constructive conversations rather than heated arguments.

Discussion Prompt:

How do you typically respond to criticism in your marriage—defensively or with gentleness? How can you both work on responding with soft words, even when discussing difficult topics? Discuss how Proverbs 15:1 encourages you to use gentle responses to foster peace and understanding in your relationship.

Prayer Focus:

Lord, we thank You for the wisdom of Your Word and for the power of gentle words. Help us to communicate with grace and patience, especially when discussing difficult issues. Teach us to respond with soft answers, turning away anger and promoting peace in our marriage. We are grateful for Your love and guidance. Amen.

Action Step:

Today, practice responding with gentle words, even if you feel defensive or frustrated. Focus on listening to your spouse and approaching the conversation with patience and love.

Marriage Minute #74: The Importance of Listening

Listening is an essential skill in marriage, one that fosters emotional intimacy and mutual understanding. James 1:19 instructs us, "Wherefore, my beloved brethren, let every man be swift to hear, slow to speak, slow to wrath." In marriage, being a good listener means paying attention not just to your spouse's words, but also to their emotions and unspoken needs.

Listening involves setting aside distractions, being present in the moment, and offering empathy and understanding. When both partners make an effort to listen deeply, it creates a safe space for vulnerability and connection. A marriage where both spouses feel heard is one where trust and emotional intimacy can thrive.

Key Truth:

> Listening in marriage fosters emotional intimacy, trust, and mutual understanding, allowing both partners to feel valued and heard.

Love's New Chapter:

As newlyweds, practice active listening by being fully present during conversations and offering empathy and understanding. Listening early in your marriage will set the foundation for strong communication.

Love in Motion:

For couples married a while, life's distractions can sometimes hinder communication. Be intentional about creating time and space for deep conversations, listening to your spouse's thoughts and feelings with care.

Love's Legacy:

After many years of marriage, you've likely learned the importance of listening. Continue to practice this skill, offering your spouse a safe space to share their heart without fear of judgment or interruption.

Legendary Lovebirds:

For those married for decades, your ability to listen deeply has likely strengthened your relationship. Keep modeling this for others, showing that a marriage where both partners feel heard is one that thrives emotionally and spiritually.

SCRIPTURE FOCUS:

"Behold, I will do a new thing; now it shall spring forth; shall ye not know it? I will even make a way in the wilderness, and rivers in the desert." – Isaiah 43:19

A Shared Moment:

Amanda and Chris were about to enter a new season of life—moving to a new city and starting fresh with new jobs. The excitement was mixed with uncertainty, and they both wondered how they would handle the transition together. According to research by Family Life, major life transitions, such as moving or career changes, can strain a marriage if not approached with intentional unity. Amanda and Chris realized they needed to rely on God's guidance as they entered this new chapter.

Scripture Exposition:

Isaiah 43:19 speaks of God doing a new thing, even in the midst of difficult or uncertain seasons. In marriage, life transitions can bring both excitement and anxiety, but God promises to make a way even in the wilderness. When couples trust in God's plan for their future, they can face transitions with confidence, knowing that He is leading them. Embracing new beginnings together strengthens the marriage, as both partners rely on God for direction, provision, and peace.

Discussion Prompt:

Are you facing any major life transitions in your marriage? How can you both trust God to guide you through these changes, relying on His provision? Discuss how Isaiah 43:19 encourages you to embrace new beginnings with faith and unity.

Prayer Focus:

Father, we thank You for the promise that You are doing a new thing in our lives and marriage. Help us to trust in Your guidance as we face life's transitions, knowing that You are making a way for us. Teach us to rely on You, embracing new beginnings with faith and unity. We are grateful for Your presence and provision. Amen.

Action Step:

Today, take time to pray together about any life transitions you are facing. Commit to trusting God's guidance and support each other through the changes, knowing He is leading you into a new season.

Marriage Minute #75: Celebrating Your Differences

Every couple is made up of two unique individuals, each with their own personality, preferences, and strengths. Romans 12:6 reminds us, "Having then gifts differing according to the grace that is given to us." In marriage, celebrating these differences means recognizing that your individuality complements one another and contributes to the beauty of your relationship.

Rather than seeing differences as obstacles, embrace them as strengths. Whether it's different perspectives, interests, or communication styles, your differences can create balance and growth in your marriage. Celebrating your spouse's unique qualities helps them feel valued and appreciated, fostering a deeper connection.

Key Truth:

> Celebrating your differences in marriage creates balance and growth, allowing both spouses to appreciate each other's unique gifts and contributions.

Love's New Chapter:
As newlyweds, you're still learning about each other's differences. Rather than trying to change your spouse, celebrate the ways in which your individuality complements each other and strengthens your relationship.

Love in Motion:
For couples married a while, differences can sometimes cause tension. Be intentional about appreciating your spouse's unique strengths and qualities, recognizing how these differences contribute to the success of your marriage.

Love's Legacy:
After many years of marriage, your differences have likely helped

create balance and depth in your relationship. Continue to celebrate the ways in which your individuality strengthens your bond.

Legendary Lovebirds:

For those married for decades, your ability to celebrate each other's differences has likely contributed to your lasting love. Keep modeling this for others, showing that a marriage where both partners are valued for their uniqueness is one that thrives.

16

NAVIGATING DISAGREEMENTS ABOUT PARENTING: PROVERBS 22:6 FOR GUIDING YOUR CHILDREN

SCRIPTURE FOCUS:

"Train up a child in the way he should go: and when he is old, he will not depart from it." – Proverbs 22:6

A Shared Moment:

Laura and David often found themselves at odds over how to discipline their children. While Laura believed in a more lenient approach, David leaned toward stricter rules. These disagreements created tension not just in their parenting but in their overall relationship. According to SYMBIS research, differing parenting styles can cause significant stress in a marriage. Laura and David realized they needed to come together and seek God's guidance in raising their children.

Scripture Exposition:

Proverbs 22:6 offers timeless wisdom for parents: we are called to train up our children in the ways of the Lord, knowing that this instruction will guide them throughout their lives. In marriage, disagreements about parenting can strain the relationship, but when couples seek God's wisdom and unite around biblical principles, they can find common ground. Parenting should be a partnership rooted in faith and guided by God's Word. By focusing on what Scripture teaches, couples can overcome their differences and work together to raise children who honor God.

Discussion Prompt:

Have you ever disagreed on parenting decisions in your marriage? How can you both come together, seeking God's wisdom and guidance for your children's upbringing? Discuss how Proverbs 22:6 encourages you to train your children in the way of the Lord and to work as a team in your parenting.

Prayer Focus:

Father, we thank You for the blessing of raising children and for the wisdom You provide. Help us to come together as parents, seeking Your guidance in every decision we make for our children. Teach us to train them in Your ways, working as a united team in our parenting. We are grateful for Your presence and love. Amen.

Action Step:

Today, have an open discussion about your parenting styles and seek to find common ground. Pray together for God's wisdom in guiding your children and commit to working as a team in raising them.

Marriage Minute #76: Keeping Romance Alive

Romance is an essential part of a thriving marriage, and it doesn't have to fade as the years go by. Song of Solomon 1:2 expresses the joy of romantic love: "Let him kiss me with the kisses of his mouth: for thy love is better than wine." In marriage, keeping romance alive means continuing to pursue each other, show affection, and create moments of connection.

Romance can be expressed in simple ways, like leaving a thoughtful note, planning a special date, or expressing affection through touch. It's about making an intentional effort to keep the spark alive, even as life's responsibilities increase. A marriage filled with romance is one that remains vibrant and joyful.

Key Truth:

> Keeping romance alive in marriage fosters emotional and physical intimacy, helping both spouses feel valued, loved, and pursued throughout the years.

Love's New Chapter:
As newlyweds, romance may come naturally, but it's important to cultivate it intentionally. Make time for dates, surprises, and affection, setting the stage for a lifetime of romantic connection.

Love in Motion:
For couples married a while, romance can sometimes take a back seat to life's demands. Reignite the romance by planning special moments of connection, whether it's a date night or a small act of affection.

Love's Legacy:

After many years of marriage, keeping romance alive may require more intentionality. Continue to pursue each other through thoughtful gestures, words of love, and shared experiences that strengthen your connection.

Legendary Lovebirds:

For those married for decades, your commitment to keeping romance alive has likely been a key to your lasting love. Keep modeling this for others, showing that romance is an essential part of a vibrant, enduring marriage.

17

HANDLING STRESSFUL SITUATIONS TOGETHER: PHILIPPIANS 4:6-7 FOR PEACE IN GOD'S PRESENCE

SCRIPTURE FOCUS:

"Be careful for nothing; but in every thing by prayer and supplication with thanksgiving let your requests be made known unto God. And the peace of God, which passeth all understanding, shall keep your hearts and minds through Christ Jesus." – Philippians 4:6-7

A Shared Moment:

Between demanding jobs, financial stress, and family responsibilities, Marissa and John were feeling overwhelmed. The stress of everyday life was taking a toll on their marriage, making them short-tempered and disconnected. According to research from Family Life, stress is one of the leading causes of marital conflict. Marissa and John realized they needed to turn to God in prayer, trusting Him to give them peace in the midst of their stressful circumstances.

Scripture Exposition:

Philippians 4:6-7 reminds us to bring our anxieties and concerns to God in prayer, trusting that His peace will guard our hearts and minds. In marriage, stressful situations can create distance, but when couples turn to God together in prayer, they experience the peace that only He can provide. God calls us to bring every worry to Him, and when we do, He offers a peace that surpasses all understanding. By relying on God's presence and peace, couples can face life's challenges with unity and faith.

Discussion Prompt:

How has stress affected your marriage, and how can you both turn to God in prayer for peace? Discuss how Philippians 4:6-7 encourages you to bring your concerns to God and trust in His peace to guard your hearts and minds.

Prayer Focus:

Lord, we thank You for the peace You offer us in every situation. Help us to turn to You in prayer when we feel overwhelmed, trusting that Your peace will guard our hearts and minds. Teach us to rely on Your presence and to handle life's stresses together with faith. We are grateful for Your love and peace. Amen.

Action Step:

Today, take time to pray together about any stressful situations you are facing. Ask God for His peace and commit to handling stress with prayer, trust, and unity.

Marriage Minute #77: Practicing Forgiveness Daily

Forgiveness is one of the most important virtues in marriage, as it allows both partners to move forward without holding on to past hurts. Colossians 3:13 instructs us, "Forbearing one another, and forgiving one another, if any man have a quarrel against any: even as Christ forgave you, so also do ye." In marriage, practicing daily forgiveness means letting go of minor grievances and choosing to extend grace to your spouse.

Forgiveness isn't about ignoring issues; it's about addressing them with love and choosing not to harbor resentment. When both spouses practice forgiveness regularly, it creates a relationship filled with grace, understanding, and emotional safety. Daily forgiveness strengthens the bond of marriage, allowing both partners to grow and thrive.

Key Truth:

> Practicing daily forgiveness in marriage fosters grace, love, and emotional safety, allowing both spouses to grow closer and heal from hurts.

Love's New Chapter:

As newlyweds, learning to forgive quickly will help you build a strong, loving foundation. Make it a habit to address issues with love and extend grace to each other when mistakes are made.

Love in Motion:

For couples married a while, past hurts can sometimes linger. Recommit to practicing daily forgiveness, letting go of minor grievances, and choosing grace over resentment.

Love's Legacy:

After many years of marriage, forgiveness has likely been a key factor in your ability to navigate challenges. Continue to practice daily forgiveness, allowing your relationship to be filled with love and understanding.

Legendary Lovebirds:

For those married for decades, your ability to forgive has likely strengthened your relationship through the years. Keep modeling this for others, showing that daily forgiveness is essential for a lasting, grace-filled marriage.

18

HONORING EACH OTHER'S STRENGTHS: ROMANS 12:10 FOR MUTUAL RESPECT

SCRIPTURE FOCUS:

"Be kindly affectioned one to another with brotherly love; in honour preferring one another." – Romans 12:10

A Shared Moment:

Sarah and Adam had very different strengths—Sarah excelled at organization and details, while Adam was more creative and spontaneous. Instead of celebrating these differences, they often found themselves frustrated with each other's approach. According to SYMBIS, learning to appreciate each other's strengths is essential for a healthy marriage. Sarah and Adam realized they needed to honor and respect what each brought to the relationship instead of focusing on their differences.

Scripture Exposition:

Romans 12:10 encourages believers to show love and honor to one another, putting others before themselves. In marriage, this means appreciating and celebrating each other's strengths instead of criticizing differences. Every couple is made up of two unique individuals, each with their own God-given talents and gifts. By honoring and preferring one another, couples can build a relationship that reflects mutual respect and love. God calls us to lift each other up, recognizing that together, our strengths complement each other and make us stronger.

Discussion Prompt:

How do you view each other's strengths in your marriage? How can you both learn to honor and celebrate those strengths instead of focusing on differences? Discuss how Romans 12:10 encourages you to honor each other with love and respect.

Prayer Focus:

Father, we thank You for the unique strengths You've given each of us. Help us to honor and respect each other's gifts, celebrating the way our strengths complement one another in our marriage. Teach us to show love and appreciation for what we each bring to the relationship. We are grateful for Your wisdom and for the love You've given us to share. Amen.

Action Step:

Today, take time to recognize and appreciate your spouse's strengths. Speak words of affirmation that celebrate what they contribute to your relationship, and focus on how your differences make you stronger as a couple.

Marriage Minute #78: Prioritizing Prayer Together

Prayer is one of the most powerful tools couples have to

strengthen their marriage. Matthew 18:20 says, "For where two or three are gathered together in my name, there am I in the midst of them." In marriage, prioritizing prayer together means making time to seek God's guidance, express gratitude, and intercede for each other.

Praying together deepens your spiritual connection and invites God's presence into your relationship. It helps both spouses align their hearts with God's will and fosters a sense of unity and peace. Whether it's a daily prayer time or spontaneous prayers throughout the day, prioritizing prayer keeps God at the center of your marriage.

Key Truth:

> Prioritizing prayer together strengthens your marriage by deepening your spiritual connection and inviting God's guidance and peace into your relationship.

Love's New Chapter:

As newlyweds, start the habit of praying together regularly. Whether it's a morning prayer or an evening devotional, prayer will help you stay spiritually connected and grounded in your marriage.

Love in Motion:

For couples married a while, prayer may sometimes get overlooked in the busyness of life. Recommit to making time for prayer, inviting God's presence and peace into your relationship.

Love's Legacy:

After many years of marriage, prayer has likely been a sustaining force in your relationship. Continue to prioritize prayer together, seeking God's guidance and relying on His strength to navigate each season.

Legendary Lovebirds:

For those married for decades, your commitment to prayer has likely been a key to your lasting love. Keep modeling this for others, showing that a marriage rooted in prayer is one that thrives through every challenge and blessing.

19

LETTING GO OF PAST HURTS: ISAIAH 43:18 FOR HEALING AND MOVING FORWARD

SCRIPTURE FOCUS:

"Remember ye not the former things, neither consider the things of old." – Isaiah 43:18

A Shared Moment:

Katie and Michael had been married for years, but old wounds from past arguments and mistakes continued to resurface, causing tension in their relationship. According to SYMBIS, holding on to past hurts can create barriers to intimacy and trust in marriage. Katie and Michael knew they needed to let go of these past pains in order to embrace the future God had for them fully.

Scripture Exposition:

Isaiah 43:18 calls believers to let go of the past and to focus on what God is doing in the present and future. In marriage, holding on to past hurts prevents true healing and creates emotional distance. God desires for couples to forgive and move forward, trusting Him for restoration and healing. By releasing old grievances and choosing forgiveness, couples can experience new life and unity in their marriage. God is always working to do something new, and by letting go of the past, couples open the door to His transformative work.

Discussion Prompt:

Are there past hurts in your marriage that still affect your relationship today? How can you both let go of those pains and focus on healing and moving forward? Discuss how Isaiah 43:18 encourages you to leave behind old grievances and trust God for restoration.

Prayer Focus:

Lord, we thank You for the healing You offer us through forgiveness. Help us to let go of any past hurts in our marriage, choosing to forgive and move forward in love. Teach us to focus on the new work You are doing in our relationship and to trust You for complete restoration. We are grateful for Your love and healing. Amen.

Action Step:

Today, have an open conversation about any past hurts that may still affect your relationship. Choose to forgive and let go, focusing on how you can move forward together with God's healing power.

Marriage Minute #79: Cultivating a Servant's Heart

In marriage, serving your spouse with a humble heart mirrors Christ's example of selfless love. Mark 10:45 says, "For even the Son of man came not to be ministered unto, but to minister, and to give his life a ransom for many." Cultivating a servant's heart means putting your spouse's needs before your own and finding joy in serving them without expecting anything in return.

A servant's heart in marriage manifests in small acts of kindness, such as helping with tasks, offering support during stressful times, and seeking to ease your spouse's burdens. When both partners embrace a servant's heart, it fosters an atmosphere of love, humility, and mutual care, deepening the bond between you.

Key Truth:

> Cultivating a servant's heart in marriage fosters love and humility, allowing both spouses to grow in their commitment to selflessly serve each other.

Love's New Chapter:

As newlyweds, practice serving each other daily, whether through small acts of kindness or offering support during stressful moments. This habit of selfless service will create a foundation of love and humility in your marriage.

Love in Motion:

For couples married a while, life's demands can sometimes make serving each other more challenging. Be intentional about finding ways to ease your spouse's burdens, serving them with love and joy.

Love's Legacy:

After many years of marriage, serving each other has likely been a key factor in your lasting relationship. Continue to serve with humility, recognizing that selfless love strengthens your bond and reflects Christ's heart.

. . .

Legendary Lovebirds:

For those married for decades, your servant's heart has likely been a source of strength and joy in your relationship. Keep modeling this for others, showing that a marriage built on mutual service is one that endures and thrives.

FINDING JOY IN THE MUNDANE: COLOSSIANS 3:23 FOR PURPOSE IN EVERY TASK

FINDING JOY IN THE MUNDANE: **Colossians 3:23 for Purpose in Every Task**

Scripture Focus:

"And whatsoever ye do, do it heartily, as to the Lord, and not unto men." – Colossians 3:23

A Shared Moment:

With busy schedules, errands, and everyday chores, Megan and Dan often felt like they were just going through the motions. The routine of daily life had drained the joy from their relationship, leaving them feeling disconnected. According to research by Family Life, finding joy in the mundane aspects of life can strengthen a marriage and foster a deeper connection. Megan and Dan realized that even the small, mundane moments could become opportunities for joy if they approached them with the right mindset.

. . .

Scripture Exposition:

Colossians 3:23 encourages believers to approach every task as if they are doing it for the Lord. In marriage, this means that even the most ordinary moments—like household chores, running errands, or managing daily responsibilities—can be filled with purpose and joy when done with love and intention. God calls couples to embrace the mundane as opportunities to serve each other and reflect His love in the small things. By finding joy in the ordinary, couples strengthen their bond and build a foundation of love that extends beyond the big moments.

Discussion Prompt:

Do you ever find it difficult to find joy in the routine aspects of marriage? How can you both approach the mundane moments with purpose and gratitude? Discuss how Colossians 3:23 encourages you to do everything with love and intention, finding joy in the ordinary.

Prayer Focus:

Father, we thank You for the purpose and joy You bring to every moment of our lives. Help us to approach the mundane aspects of marriage with gratitude and love, seeing them as opportunities to serve each other. Teach us to find joy in the small moments, knowing that they are a reflection of Your love. We are grateful for Your presence in every task. Amen.

Action Step:

Today, choose one routine task—whether it's cooking dinner, doing laundry, or running an errand—and approach it with joy and love, knowing that even the ordinary can strengthen your marriage.

Marriage Minute #80: Embracing Patience in Parenting

Parenting brings unique challenges, and maintaining patience is crucial for both partners. Proverbs 14:29 reminds us, "He that is slow to wrath is of great understanding: but he that is hasty of spirit exalteth folly." In marriage, embracing patience with your spouse during the trials of parenting means supporting each other, remaining calm during difficult moments, and extending grace when mistakes are made.

Patience in parenting involves being understanding when your spouse is overwhelmed, offering help when needed, and recognizing that both of you are learning and growing together as parents. When both partners practice patience in their parenting roles, it creates a nurturing environment for the entire family, allowing love and growth to flourish.

Key Truth:

> Patience in parenting creates a supportive, loving environment, fostering understanding and grace between spouses as they navigate the challenges of raising children.

Love's New Chapter:

As newlyweds, you may be preparing for parenthood. Start practicing patience now by supporting each other and giving grace when things don't go as planned. This will help build a strong foundation for your family.

Love in Motion:

For couples married a while, parenting can bring added stress and challenges. Be intentional about practicing patience with each other, offering understanding and help during difficult times.

Love's Legacy:

After many years of marriage, patience in parenting has likely been a key to raising your children with love and grace. Continue to support each other, recognizing that patience strengthens both your marriage and your family.

Legendary Lovebirds:

For those married for decades, your ability to practice patience in parenting has likely shaped a loving, secure family. Keep modeling this for others, showing that patience is essential for building a strong and nurturing home.

21

WORKING THROUGH DISAGREEMENTS ABOUT FINANCES: LUKE 16:11 FOR FAITHFULNESS IN STEWARDSHIP

SCRIPTURE FOCUS:

"If therefore ye have not been faithful in the unrighteous mammon, who will commit to your trust the true riches?" – Luke 16:11

A Shared Moment:

Finances were a constant source of tension between Julie and Greg. They often disagreed on how to budget, save, and spend, which led to arguments and stress. According to Barna research, financial disagreements are one of the top reasons for marital conflict. Julie and Greg knew they needed to get on the same page financially and work toward faithful stewardship of their resources.

Scripture Exposition:

Luke 16:11 speaks to the importance of being faithful with the resources God has given us. In marriage, financial stewardship is not just about making ends meet but about honoring God with how we manage our money. When couples are faithful in their financial decisions, they create a foundation of trust and unity. God calls us to be wise stewards, and when both spouses work together toward financial faithfulness, they experience peace and blessings in their marriage. Aligning financial decisions with biblical principles strengthens both the marriage and the family's future.

Discussion Prompt:

Have financial disagreements caused tension in your marriage? How can you both work toward faithful stewardship, honoring God with your financial decisions? Discuss how Luke 16:11 encourages you to be wise and faithful stewards of the resources God has entrusted to you.

Prayer Focus:

Lord, we thank You for the resources You have given us and for the opportunity to be faithful stewards. Help us to come together in our financial decisions, honoring You with how we manage our money. Teach us to work as a team, prioritizing faithfulness and unity in our finances. We are grateful for Your wisdom and provision. Amen.

Action Step:

Today, take time to review your financial situation together. Pray for wisdom and unity in making financial decisions, and commit to working as a team to honor God with your resources.

Marriage Minute #81: Protecting Your Marriage with Boundaries

Setting boundaries in marriage is crucial for maintaining

emotional and relational health. Proverbs 25:17 warns, "Withdraw thy foot from thy neighbour's house; lest he be weary of thee, and so hate thee." In marriage, boundaries protect your relationship from outside influences, distractions, and potential sources of conflict, keeping the focus on your connection with each other.

Healthy boundaries may include protecting your time together, managing external relationships, or setting limits on media and technology use. These boundaries help prevent distractions and misunderstandings, ensuring that both partners feel secure and prioritized. A marriage with clear boundaries fosters trust, intimacy, and emotional safety.

Key Truth:

> Protecting your marriage with healthy boundaries strengthens your relationship by fostering trust, intimacy, and emotional security.

Love's New Chapter:

As newlyweds, start setting healthy boundaries early to protect your relationship. Be intentional about creating time for each other and managing external influences that could disrupt your connection.

Love in Motion:

For couples married a while, boundaries may sometimes be overlooked as life's demands increase. Revisit your boundaries to ensure they are still protecting your relationship and keeping your marriage a priority.

. . .

Love's Legacy:

After many years of marriage, healthy boundaries have likely helped maintain balance and peace in your relationship. Continue to uphold these boundaries, ensuring that your marriage remains strong and secure.

Legendary Lovebirds:

For those married for decades, your healthy boundaries have likely played a significant role in your lasting relationship. Keep modeling this for younger couples, showing that boundaries are a vital part of a strong, enduring marriage.

22

CELEBRATING EACH OTHER'S ACCOMPLISHMENTS: ROMANS 12:15 FOR REJOICING TOGETHER

SCRIPTURE FOCUS:

"Rejoice with them that do rejoice, and weep with them that weep." – Romans 12:15

A Shared Moment:

When Brian received a promotion at work, his wife, Claire, felt happy for him, but she also felt a twinge of jealousy because her own career hadn't been progressing as she'd hoped. According to research from SYMBIS, learning to genuinely celebrate each other's accomplishments without comparison strengthens a marriage. Claire and Brian realized they needed to focus on lifting each other up rather than allowing insecurity to creep in.

Scripture Exposition:

Romans 12:15 calls us to rejoice with those who rejoice and weep with those who weep. In marriage, this means truly sharing in each other's victories and joys, without letting jealousy or insecurity diminish our support. God calls couples to lift each other up, to celebrate each other's accomplishments, and to stand by one another in moments of success and challenge. By choosing to celebrate each other's wins, couples strengthen their bond and create a relationship where both partners feel valued and supported.

Discussion Prompt:

Do you genuinely celebrate your spouse's accomplishments, or do feelings of jealousy sometimes arise? How can you both work on rejoicing with each other, no matter the season? Discuss how Romans 12:15 encourages you to celebrate each other's victories without comparison or insecurity.

Prayer Focus:

Father, we thank You for the unique gifts and opportunities You have given each of us. Help us to celebrate each other's accomplishments, lifting each other up without comparison or jealousy. Teach us to rejoice together in moments of success and to support one another with genuine love and joy. We are grateful for Your grace and guidance. Amen.

Action Step:

Today, take time to celebrate one of your spouse's recent accomplishments. Whether it's big or small, express your pride and joy in their success, and focus on lifting each other up.

Marriage Minute #82: Gratitude for Each Other's Contributions

Gratitude is a powerful way to affirm your spouse's value in your marriage. 1 Thessalonians 5:18 tells us, "In every thing give thanks:

for this is the will of God in Christ Jesus concerning you." In marriage, expressing gratitude for your spouse's contributions—whether big or small—helps create an atmosphere of appreciation and respect.

Gratitude fosters love and emotional connection, reminding both partners that their efforts are seen and valued. Whether it's thanking your spouse for helping with daily tasks, acknowledging their hard work, or simply appreciating their presence, gratitude strengthens the bond between you and creates a positive dynamic in your marriage.

Key Truth:

Expressing gratitude for each other's contributions fosters appreciation, love, and respect, strengthening the emotional connection between spouses.

Love's New Chapter:

As newlyweds, make it a habit to express gratitude for your spouse's efforts, whether they are small daily tasks or larger contributions. This practice will build a strong foundation of appreciation and respect.

Love in Motion:

For couples married a while, life's demands can sometimes make it easy to overlook gratitude. Be intentional about thanking your spouse for their efforts, reminding them that their contributions are valued and appreciated.

Love's Legacy:

After many years of marriage, gratitude has likely played a significant role in maintaining a positive, loving relationship. Continue to express appreciation for your spouse's efforts, creating a marriage filled with love and respect.

Legendary Lovebirds:

For those married for decades, your habit of expressing gratitude has likely strengthened your relationship through the years. Keep modeling this for others, showing that gratitude is a key to building a lasting, loving marriage.

23

REAFFIRMING YOUR COMMITMENT IN MARRIAGE: RUTH 1:16 FOR LOYALTY AND FAITHFULNESS

SCRIPTURE FOCUS:

"And Ruth said, Intreat me not to leave thee, or to return from following after thee: for whither thou goest, I will go; and where thou lodgest, I will lodge: thy people shall be my people, and thy God my God." – Ruth 1:16

A Shared Moment:

After 15 years of marriage, Rebecca and Jacob realized they had drifted apart emotionally. Life's demands had taken a toll, and they both felt disconnected. According to Family Life research, regular reaffirmation of commitment helps couples stay emotionally and spiritually connected. Rebecca and Jacob knew they needed to intentionally remind each other of their love and commitment, renewing their dedication to one another.

Scripture Exposition:

Ruth 1:16 is a powerful declaration of loyalty and commitment, originally between Ruth and Naomi, but it also provides a beautiful parallel for marriage. In marriage, reaffirming our commitment to each other strengthens the bond of love and loyalty that keeps us connected through life's ups and downs. God calls couples to stand by each other, remaining faithful and loyal, just as He remains faithful to us. By regularly reaffirming this commitment, couples can renew their emotional connection and strengthen their marriage.

Discussion Prompt:

Have you ever felt emotionally disconnected in your marriage? How can you both reaffirm your commitment to one another and renew your dedication? Discuss how Ruth 1:16 encourages loyalty and faithfulness in your relationship.

Prayer Focus:

Lord, we thank You for the commitment we made to each other in marriage and for the faithfulness You show us every day. Help us to reaffirm our love and commitment, staying loyal to one another through every season of life. Teach us to be faithful to our vows, and strengthen our emotional connection. We are grateful for Your guidance and love. Amen.

Action Step:

Today, take a moment to reaffirm your commitment to each other. Speak words of love and dedication, reminding your spouse that you are fully committed to them and to your marriage.

Marriage Minute #83: Balancing Individual and Shared Interests

A healthy marriage includes both individual growth and shared experiences. Philippians 2:4 encourages us, "Look not every man on his own things, but every man also on the things of others." In marriage, balancing individual and shared interests allows both spouses to pursue their personal passions while also prioritizing the relationship.

Balancing individual and shared interests involves supporting your spouse's personal goals and hobbies while also nurturing shared experiences that strengthen your bond. When both partners feel valued in their individual pursuits and connected in their shared life, the marriage becomes richer and more fulfilling.

Key Truth:

> Balancing individual and shared interests in marriage fosters personal growth and strengthens the bond between spouses, creating a fulfilling, well-rounded relationship.

Love's New Chapter:
As newlyweds, begin balancing individual and shared interests by supporting each other's goals and finding activities you can enjoy together. This balance will help create a strong, fulfilling marriage.

Love in Motion:
For couples married a while, it's important to revisit how you balance individual and shared interests. Encourage your spouse's personal growth while also making time for experiences that nurture your relationship.

. . .

Love's Legacy:

After many years of marriage, you've likely learned how to balance personal growth with shared experiences. Continue to support your spouse's individual pursuits while also finding new ways to connect as a couple.

Legendary Lovebirds:

For those married for decades, your ability to balance individual and shared interests has likely contributed to your lasting relationship. Keep modeling this for others, showing that personal growth and shared experiences create a strong, vibrant marriage.

24

NAVIGATING UNMET EXPECTATIONS: EPHESIANS 4:2-3 FOR HUMILITY AND UNITY

SCRIPTURE FOCUS:

"With all lowliness and meekness, with longsuffering, forbearing one another in love; Endeavouring to keep the unity of the Spirit in the bond of peace." – Ephesians 4:2-3

A Shared Moment:

Emily had always dreamed that marriage would look a certain way, but as the years went on, she found herself disappointed that things didn't turn out exactly as she imagined. Her husband, Mark, felt the pressure of her unmet expectations, which created tension in their relationship. According to research from SYMBIS, unmet expectations are a common cause of frustration in marriage. Emily and Mark realized they needed to work on communicating their needs and adjusting their expectations with humility and grace.

Scripture Exposition:

Ephesians 4:2-3 calls believers to approach relationships with humility, patience, and love, seeking to maintain unity. In marriage, unmet expectations can lead to disappointment and division, but this passage encourages couples to bear with one another in love, understanding that no one is perfect. When couples communicate openly and approach their marriage with humility, they can overcome unmet expectations and find unity in the Spirit. God calls us to love and forbear with each other, seeking peace and unity, even when things don't go as planned.

Discussion Prompt:

Have unmet expectations ever caused frustration in your marriage? How can you both approach your relationship with humility and love, adjusting expectations and seeking unity? Discuss how Ephesians 4:2-3 encourages you to bear with one another and maintain peace in your marriage.

Prayer Focus:

Father, we thank You for the love and patience You show us daily. Help us to approach our marriage with humility, adjusting our expectations with grace and understanding. Teach us to communicate openly and to bear with each other in love, seeking unity and peace. We are grateful for Your presence and guidance in our relationship. Amen.

Action Step:

Today, have a conversation about any unmet expectations that may have caused frustration. Approach the discussion with humility and love, working together to adjust expectations and maintain unity in your marriage.

Marriage Minute #84: Being Quick to Forgive

In marriage, forgiveness is not just a one-time act but a daily practice. Ephesians 4:32 instructs us, "And be ye kind one to another, tenderhearted, forgiving one another, even as God for Christ's sake hath forgiven you." Being quick to forgive means not holding grudges or letting resentment build but choosing grace and understanding in every conflict.

Quick forgiveness creates a culture of grace in marriage, where both partners feel safe to be vulnerable and make mistakes without fear of rejection. It also prevents bitterness from taking root and strengthens the bond of trust. When both spouses are quick to forgive, the marriage becomes a place of healing, growth, and unconditional love.

Key Truth:

> Being quick to forgive in marriage fosters grace, trust, and emotional safety, allowing both spouses to grow closer and heal from mistakes.

Love's New Chapter:

As newlyweds, practice quick forgiveness early by letting go of small grievances and choosing grace over resentment. This will help create a marriage filled with love and understanding.

Love in Motion:

For couples married a while, past hurts can sometimes linger. Be intentional about practicing quick forgiveness, letting go of resentment, and choosing to extend grace when conflicts arise.

. . .

Love's Legacy:

After many years of marriage, quick forgiveness has likely played a key role in keeping your relationship strong. Continue to offer grace and understanding, creating a marriage that is filled with love and emotional safety.

Legendary Lovebirds:

For those married for decades, your ability to forgive quickly has likely strengthened your relationship over the years. Keep modeling this for others, showing that quick forgiveness is essential for a lasting, grace-filled marriage.

EMBRACING CHANGE IN MARRIAGE: 2 CORINTHIANS 5:17 FOR NEW BEGINNINGS

EMBRACING CHANGE IN MARRIAGE: **2 Corinthians 5:17 for New Beginnings**

Scripture Focus:

"Therefore if any man be in Christ, he is a new creature: old things are passed away; behold, all things are become new." – 2 Corinthians 5:17

A Shared Moment:

David and Lucy had been married for 20 years, and with the kids now out of the house, they found themselves in a new season of life. While excited about the future, they also felt uncertain about how to navigate the changes that came with this new chapter. According to Family Life, embracing change together helps couples grow closer during transitional seasons. David and Lucy realized they needed to embrace this new beginning with hope, trusting God to guide them through the changes.

. . .

Scripture Exposition:

2 Corinthians 5:17 speaks of the transformative power of being in Christ, where old things pass away, and all things become new. In marriage, seasons of change are inevitable, but God calls couples to embrace these changes with faith and trust in His plan. When both partners trust in Christ, they can face new beginnings with confidence, knowing that God is making all things new in their marriage. Embracing change together creates opportunities for growth, deeper connection, and renewed purpose in the relationship.

Discussion Prompt:

Are you currently facing any changes in your marriage? How can you both embrace these changes with hope and trust in God's plan? Discuss how 2 Corinthians 5:17 encourages you to embrace new beginnings and allow God to make all things new in your marriage.

Prayer Focus:

Lord, we thank You for the new beginnings You bring into our lives and marriage. Help us to embrace the changes we face with hope and trust in Your plan. Teach us to grow closer to each other during seasons of transition, knowing that You are making all things new. We are grateful for Your guidance and love. Amen.

Action Step:

Today, talk about any changes you are currently navigating in your marriage. Pray together for wisdom and strength, trusting God to guide you through this new season and to bring renewal to your relationship.

Marriage Minute #85: The Gift of Time

Time is one of the most valuable gifts you can give in marriage. Psalm 90:12 teaches us, "So teach us to number our days, that we may apply our hearts unto wisdom." In marriage, spending quality time together strengthens your bond, deepens your emotional connection, and creates lasting memories.

The gift of time doesn't always require elaborate plans; it can be as simple as a shared meal, a walk, or a conversation without distractions. When both partners prioritize spending time together, it fosters a sense of closeness and intimacy. The moments spent together, whether big or small, build a strong foundation for a lasting, loving marriage.

Key Truth:

Giving the gift of time in marriage strengthens your bond and deepens emotional intimacy, creating a relationship filled with love and connection.

Love's New Chapter:

As newlyweds, make time for each other a priority, even in the midst of life's demands. Whether it's a date night or a quiet evening at home, the time you spend together will strengthen your connection.

Love in Motion:

For couples married a while, life's busyness can sometimes make quality time scarce. Recommit to giving the gift of time, making an effort to spend meaningful moments together regularly.

· : ·

Love's Legacy:

After many years of marriage, the time you've spent together has likely created countless memories. Continue to prioritize quality time, ensuring that your connection remains strong and your love deepens with each passing year.

Legendary Lovebirds:

For those married for decades, your commitment to spending time together has likely been a key to your lasting love. Keep modeling this for younger couples, showing that time is one of the greatest gifts you can give to your spouse.

CELEBRATING MILESTONES IN MARRIAGE: PSALM 126:3 FOR JOY IN GOD'S BLESSINGS

SCRIPTURE FOCUS:

"The Lord hath done great things for us; whereof we are glad." – Psalm 126:3

A Shared Moment:

John and Marie recently celebrated their 10th wedding anniversary, but in the busyness of life, they hadn't taken the time to reflect on all the blessings they had experienced together. According to Family Life, celebrating milestones in marriage helps couples reflect on God's faithfulness and strengthens their bond. John and Marie realized they needed to take a moment to rejoice in the great things God had done in their lives and marriage.

Scripture Exposition:

Psalm 126:3 reminds us to take joy in the great things God has done. In marriage, it's important to celebrate the milestones—whether big or small—that mark the journey together. When couples take time to reflect on God's blessings and faithfulness, they are reminded of His goodness and provision. God calls us to rejoice in His work in our lives, and by celebrating milestones, couples strengthen their bond and create lasting memories. Gratitude and joy deepen the connection and help couples focus on the good that God has done.

Discussion Prompt:

Have you taken time to celebrate the milestones in your marriage? How can you both reflect on God's blessings and rejoice in His faithfulness? Discuss how Psalm 126:3 encourages you to take joy in the great things God has done in your marriage.

Prayer Focus:

Father, we thank You for the many blessings You have brought into our marriage. Help us to take time to reflect on the milestones we've reached and to rejoice in Your faithfulness. Teach us to celebrate the good things You have done and to find joy in every season of our journey together. We are grateful for Your love and provision. Amen.

Action Step:

Today, take time to celebrate a milestone in your marriage. Whether it's a wedding anniversary, a special memory, or an achievement, reflect on God's faithfulness and rejoice in the blessings He has brought into your relationship.

Marriage Minute #86: Celebrating Small Wins

In marriage, it's important to celebrate not only the big milestones but also the small victories along the way. Zechariah 4:10 encourages us, "For who hath despised the day of small things?" Celebrating small wins—whether it's a shared accomplishment, overcoming a challenge, or simply making it through a tough day—fosters joy and gratitude in your marriage.

Acknowledging these small moments of success reminds you and your spouse that growth and progress are always happening, even in the day-to-day routine. Celebrating small wins brings positivity into your relationship and encourages both partners to continue building and supporting each other.

Key Truth:

> Celebrating small wins in marriage fosters gratitude, joy, and a sense of shared accomplishment, helping both partners stay positive and connected.

Love's New Chapter:

As newlyweds, take time to celebrate the small wins in your relationship. Whether it's learning something new about each other or navigating a challenge together, these moments will strengthen your bond and bring joy to your journey.

Love in Motion:

For couples married a while, it's easy to overlook the small victories in the busyness of life. Be intentional about acknowledging and celebrating the little moments that bring progress, joy, or relief to your relationship.

Love's Legacy:

After many years of marriage, celebrating small wins may have helped sustain your joy and connection. Continue to find reasons to celebrate, recognizing that each small step contributes to the strength of your marriage.

Legendary Lovebirds:

For those married for decades, your ability to celebrate small wins has likely been a source of ongoing joy in your relationship. Keep modeling this for others, showing that even the little victories matter in a long-lasting marriage.

BALANCING WORK AND MARRIAGE: COLOSSIANS 3:17 FOR A CHRIST-CENTERED LIFE

SCRIPTURE FOCUS:

"And whatsoever ye do in word or deed, do all in the name of the Lord Jesus, giving thanks to God and the Father by him." – Colossians 3:17

A Shared Moment:

Ben had been working long hours to provide for his family, but his wife, Sarah, felt neglected as his attention was mostly focused on work. Balancing work and marriage had become a struggle for them. According to research by Barna, work-related stress can strain a marriage if not managed properly. Ben and Sarah realized they needed to prioritize their relationship while maintaining their professional responsibilities.

Scripture Exposition:

Colossians 3:17 calls us to do everything in the name of the Lord, giving thanks to God. In marriage, balancing work and personal life can be challenging, but God calls us to approach every area of life—

including our careers—with a Christ-centered perspective. By ensuring that work, marriage, and family are all done in His name and with a thankful heart, couples can create harmony. When both spouses honor God in their work and home life, they experience peace and balance.

Discussion Prompt:

Do you struggle with balancing work and your marriage? How can you both ensure that your relationship remains a priority while managing your responsibilities? Discuss how Colossians 3:17 encourages you to invite Christ into every aspect of your life and marriage.

Prayer Focus:

Lord, we thank You for the opportunity to work and provide for our family. Help us to balance our work and marriage, keeping You at the center of everything we do. Teach us to honor You in our responsibilities and to prioritize our relationship, giving thanks for Your provision. We are grateful for Your wisdom and guidance. Amen.

Action Step:

Today, discuss ways to create more balance between work and marriage. Make a plan to carve out intentional time for each other, ensuring that your relationship remains strong even in the midst of busy schedules.

Marriage Minute #87: Speaking Kindly, Even in Conflict

Conflict is inevitable in any marriage, but how you handle it can make all the difference. Proverbs 15:1 reminds us, "A soft answer turneth away wrath: but grievous words stir up anger." In marriage, speaking kindly—even during disagreements—helps prevent conflict from escalating and fosters an atmosphere of respect and understanding.

When you choose gentle words instead of harsh ones, it creates a safe space for open communication and helps both partners feel heard and respected. Kindness doesn't mean avoiding the issue, but rather addressing it with love and patience. Speaking kindly during conflict helps resolve the issue while strengthening the emotional bond between you.

Key Truth:

Speaking kindly during conflict fosters respect, patience, and emotional safety, allowing both spouses to address issues without damaging their relationship.

Love's New Chapter:

As newlyweds, you're still learning how to navigate conflict. Practice speaking kindly during disagreements, using gentle words to communicate your feelings without causing unnecessary hurt.

Love in Motion:

For couples married a while, it's easy to let frustration slip into harsh words during conflict. Recommit to speaking kindly, even when tensions are high, knowing that gentle words foster resolution and understanding.

Love's Legacy:

After many years of marriage, speaking kindly during conflict has likely helped you navigate many challenges. Continue to practice this, using love and patience to resolve disagreements in a way that strengthens your marriage.

Legendary Lovebirds:

For those married for decades, your ability to speak kindly during conflict has likely played a significant role in your lasting relationship. Keep modeling this for others, showing that kindness during disagreements helps build a marriage based on respect and love.

OVERCOMING FEELINGS OF INADEQUACY: 2 CORINTHIANS 12:9 FOR GOD'S STRENGTH IN WEAKNESS

SCRIPTURE FOCUS:

"And he said unto me, My grace is sufficient for thee: for my strength is made perfect in weakness." – 2 Corinthians 12:9

A Shared Moment:

Jennifer often felt like she wasn't enough—whether it was as a wife, mother, or even in her career. These feelings of inadequacy weighed on her heart and affected her confidence in her marriage. According to SYMBIS, many individuals struggle with feelings of inadequacy, which can create emotional distance in marriage. Jennifer realized she needed to trust in God's grace and strength, rather than relying solely on herself.

Scripture Exposition:

2 Corinthians 12:9 reminds us that God's grace is sufficient and that His strength is made perfect in our weakness. In marriage, when one partner feels inadequate, it can lead to insecurity and emotional distance. However, God's promise is that His grace is enough to fill in

the gaps where we fall short. When couples rely on God's strength instead of their own, they experience peace and confidence, knowing that He will sustain them through every weakness.

Discussion Prompt:

Have you or your spouse ever felt inadequate in your marriage? How can you both trust in God's grace and strength to overcome those feelings? Discuss how 2 Corinthians 12:9 encourages you to rely on God's strength in the areas where you feel weak.

Prayer Focus:

Father, we thank You for Your grace, which is always sufficient for us. Help us to trust in Your strength when we feel inadequate, knowing that You are with us in every weakness. Teach us to rely on Your power in our marriage, growing stronger together as we trust in You. We are grateful for Your love and grace. Amen.

Action Step:

Today, take time to encourage each other, acknowledging areas where you may feel inadequate. Pray together, trusting that God's grace is enough to strengthen your marriage in those areas of weakness.

Marriage Minute #88: The Importance of Laughter

Laughter is often called "the best medicine," and it's certainly true in marriage. Proverbs 17:22 reminds us, "A merry heart doeth good like a medicine." In marriage, finding moments to laugh together helps relieve stress, build emotional intimacy, and bring joy to your relationship.

Laughter can break the tension during stressful times and create memories that strengthen your bond. Whether it's sharing a joke, watching a funny movie, or simply finding humor in the little things, laughter helps keep your relationship lighthearted and positive. A marriage filled with laughter is one that thrives on joy and connection.

Key Truth:

> Laughter in marriage relieves stress and fosters emotional intimacy, bringing joy and positivity to your relationship.

Love's New Chapter:
As newlyweds, laughter will come naturally as you explore life together. Keep finding moments to laugh, whether it's through shared experiences, funny stories, or simply enjoying each other's company.

Love in Motion:
For couples married a while, life's demands can sometimes make it harder to find moments of joy. Be intentional about laughing together, even during challenging times, as laughter strengthens your bond and lifts your spirits.

Love's Legacy:
After many years of marriage, laughter has likely been a key to maintaining your connection and joy. Continue to find reasons to laugh together, recognizing that laughter is one of the simplest ways to keep your relationship thriving.

. . .

Legendary Lovebirds:

For those married for decades, your ability to laugh together has likely been a source of joy in your relationship. Keep modeling this for younger couples, showing that laughter is essential for a joyful, lasting marriage.

SCRIPTURE FOCUS:

"Restore unto me the joy of thy salvation; and uphold me with thy free spirit." – Psalm 51:12

A Shared Moment:

After years of marriage, the spark that once brought joy to Samantha and Tom's relationship had dimmed. They still loved each other, but the busyness of life had caused them to lose the joy they once shared. According to Family Life, joy is essential for maintaining a thriving marriage, yet it often fades without intentional effort. Samantha and Tom knew they needed to ask God to restore the joy they had once known.

Scripture Exposition:

Psalm 51:12 is a prayer for God to restore the joy of salvation. In marriage, joy can diminish over time, but God desires to renew it. Joy in marriage comes from a heart that is connected to God and filled with gratitude for His blessings. When couples seek God's restoration and joy, He renews their hearts and fills their relationship with gladness. By focusing on God's grace and love, couples can rediscover the joy that first brought them together.

Discussion Prompt:

Has joy faded in your marriage over time? How can you both ask God to restore that joy and bring renewed gladness to your relationship? Discuss how Psalm 51:12 encourages you to seek God's restoration for your marriage.

Prayer Focus:

Lord, we thank You for the joy You bring to our lives and marriage. Help us to seek Your restoration, renewing the joy that may have faded over time. Teach us to focus on Your love and grace, and to rediscover the gladness that first brought us together. We are grateful for Your presence and joy in our marriage. Amen.

Action Step:

Today, do something joyful together as a couple—whether it's going for a walk, enjoying a hobby, or reminiscing about joyful memories. Ask God to restore and renew the joy in your marriage.

Marriage Minute #89: Practicing Empathy

Empathy is the ability to understand and share your spouse's feelings, offering support and comfort. Romans 12:15 instructs us, "Rejoice with them that do rejoice, and weep with them that weep." In marriage, practicing empathy means being present with your spouse in both their joys and their struggles, offering a listening ear and a compassionate heart.

Empathy builds emotional intimacy and helps both partners feel valued and understood. When you take the time to truly listen and put yourself in your spouse's shoes, it strengthens your connection and fosters a deeper sense of trust and unity.

Key Truth:

> Practicing empathy in marriage strengthens emotional intimacy and fosters a deeper connection, allowing both spouses to feel valued and understood.

Love's New Chapter:

As newlyweds, empathy will help you understand each other's feelings and navigate new experiences. Practice listening carefully and offering support during both joyful and challenging times.

Love in Motion:

For couples married a while, empathy can sometimes be overshadowed by life's demands. Be intentional about practicing empathy, offering your spouse your full attention and understanding during moments of need.

Love's Legacy:

After many years of marriage, empathy has likely played a significant role in your emotional connection. Continue to practice empathy, recognizing that it deepens your bond and strengthens your relationship.

. . .

Legendary Lovebirds:

For those married for decades, your ability to empathize with each other has likely been a source of strength in your relationship. Keep modeling this for others, showing that empathy creates a marriage filled with love, understanding, and support.

SCRIPTURE FOCUS:

"Therefore whosoever heareth these sayings of mine, and doeth them, I will liken him unto a wise man, which built his house upon a rock." – Matthew 7:24

A Shared Moment:

Emma and Will had been through some tough times in their marriage—financial struggles, disagreements, and misunderstandings —but they knew that their faith in Christ had always been the foundation that held them together. According to Barna research, marriages that are built on a shared faith in Christ tend to be stronger and more resilient. Emma and Will knew that keeping Christ at the center of their marriage was the key to enduring every storm.

Scripture Exposition:

Matthew 7:24 speaks of the importance of building our lives on the solid foundation of Christ's teachings. In marriage, Christ must be the cornerstone upon which the relationship is built. When couples build their marriage on Christ's love, grace, and wisdom, they create a foundation that can withstand any storm. God calls us to hear and apply His Word in every aspect of life, including marriage, ensuring that our relationship is firmly rooted in His truth. By prioritizing Christ in marriage, couples can face challenges with confidence and unity.

Discussion Prompt:

Is your marriage built on the solid foundation of Christ? How can you both work to keep Him at the center of your relationship? Discuss how Matthew 7:24 encourages you to build your marriage on Christ's teachings for a strong and lasting foundation.

Prayer Focus:

Father, we thank You for being the solid rock upon which we can build our lives and marriage. Help us to keep You at the center of our relationship, building our marriage on the foundation of Your Word and love. Teach us to trust in You in every situation, knowing that You will hold us steady through every storm. We are grateful for Your presence and guidance. Amen.

Action Step:

Today, talk about ways you can strengthen your Christ-centered foundation. Pray together, committing to keep Christ at the heart of your marriage, and seek opportunities to grow in faith as a couple.

Marriage Minute #90: The Strength of Endurance

Marriage is a lifelong journey, and enduring through the ups and downs requires commitment, patience, and faith. Galatians 6:9

encourages us, "And let us not be weary in well doing: for in due season we shall reap, if we faint not." Endurance in marriage means staying committed through both the joyful moments and the difficult seasons, trusting that God is at work in your relationship.

Endurance is built through prayer, perseverance, and mutual support. When both spouses are committed to weathering life's challenges together, the marriage grows stronger and more resilient. Endurance creates a deep sense of trust and unity, allowing both partners to grow together in love and faith.

Key Truth:

> The strength of endurance in marriage fosters resilience, trust, and unity, allowing both spouses to navigate life's challenges with faith and commitment.

Love's New Chapter:

As newlyweds, begin building endurance by supporting each other through the early challenges of marriage. Trust that your commitment to one another will carry you through both the highs and lows of your journey together.

Love in Motion:

For couples married a while, endurance may already be part of your story. Continue to rely on each other and on God's strength, knowing that your perseverance will deepen your bond and lead to greater joy.

Love's Legacy:

After many years of marriage, endurance has likely been a key factor in your ability to navigate life's challenges. Continue to lean on each other during difficult seasons, trusting that your endurance will strengthen your relationship.

Legendary Lovebirds:

For those married for decades, your endurance through both the highs and lows has likely testified to your love and commitment. Keep modeling this for others, showing that a marriage built on endurance thrives through every season of life.

www.ingramcontent.com/pod-product-compliance
Lightning Source LLC
Chambersburg PA
CBHW051839130726
47987CB00002B/613